Loves of Our Lives

Loves of Our Lives

POEMS FOR HOPEFUL HEARTS

JOSIE BALKA

Simon Element

NEW YORK AMSTERDAM/ANTWERP LONDON
TORONTO SYDNEY/MELBOURNE NEW DELHI

SIMON
ELEMENT

An Imprint of Simon & Schuster, LLC
1230 Avenue of the Americas
New York, NY 10020

First Simon Element hardcover edition December 2025

SIMON ELEMENT is a trademark of Simon & Schuster, LLC

For information about special discounts for bulk purchases, please contact Simon & Schuster Special Sales at 1-866-506-1949 or business@simonandschuster.com.

The Simon & Schuster Speakers Bureau can bring authors to your live event. For more information or to book an event, contact the Simon & Schuster Speakers Bureau at 1-866-248-3049 or visit our website at www.simonspeakers.com.

Interior design by Laura Levatino

Manufactured in the United States of America

10 9 8 7 6 5 4 3 2 1

Library of Congress Control Number: 2025947931

ISBN 978-1-6682-0990-5
ISBN 978-1-6682-0992-9 (ebook)

To everyone I've ever loved, I meant it.
Thank you for letting me get to know my favorite feeling.

CONTENTS

Loves of
Our Lives

INTRODUCTION

Some people give you Sunday mornings, and some late Friday nights
Some things end without a warning, and some without surprise
Some people keep you on your toes, and some keep you laid flat
Sometimes people find love in an instant

(It took me years to believe in that)

Sometimes love keeps you level and kind, and sometimes
   it makes you cruel
It can keep you very by the book, or breaking all the rules
It can leave you coming home with a big smile on your face
Or crying in a taxi when you're leaving someone's place
You might go out on a limb and find that love prevails
Or just barely survive it, *but you're here to tell the tale*
And in the end, we're all willing to lose our common sense
To take part in one of life's most outrageous experiments
And even though it leaves us all with heaps and piles of healing
We're all only humans,

Just searching for a feeling.

ROMANTIC LOVE

or, The Ones Who Really Felt Like the One

To be in love with anything *is to be in love*
Because love is meant to be equally as fulfilling
No matter what it's directed at
So be in love with your life in every way that you possibly can
And let it be known that *that is what being in love is*
Be in love with trying new recipes and taking the long way home
And coffee that's exactly how you like it every morning
Be in love with the last album your favorite artist released
A book you read recently, or your weekly trip to the grocery store
Be in love with rainy days
A really good workout, your skin-care routine
Your favorite outfit
Be in love with everything you love
Immerse yourself in it
Fall hard for it
And be so sure of it that you never wonder if it's going leave
Feel the type of joy you think you only get to have when you're in love
Because you are
This is what love is all about
And to let yourself do all your favorite things
And feel *that* deeply about them
Is the most profound form of being loved in return
Because you are constantly surrounded by all of it
If you let yourself fall in love with *everything you love*
You are always in love

And what a beautiful way to be

The one who loves you will not make you spend a day wondering
Whether they love you or not
You will know the whole time
The one who loves you will not keep you a secret
They will tell everyone that they are the one who loves you
They will tell their friends
And they will tell mountaintops and strangers
And they will tell you, too
Not in code or a language you don't understand
Not only with actions but with *those exact words*
The one who loves you will only make you wait the perfect
     amount of time
And it won't even feel like waiting
It will feel like time flying
The one who loves you will never make you scared that the end
     is coming
Because new chapters will keep beginning and beginning
And they will make any endings feel like turning corners instead
     of closing doors
They will challenge you, because that's life
And they will also change for you, like you will change for them
But only in ways that make sense
Because they are the one who loves you
They will love you in a way that *feels* like love
You will know
And during moments when you are pushing them away
You will find their feet are glued to the ground in front of you
Because they are not going anywhere

And one day, years from the start, you will wake up beside
    the one who loves you
And you will realize you knew all along
Because they never for a moment treated you like they didn't
When the one who loves you loves you, you will know

―――――――

I met you in the summer and all I could do was hope I'd have the
    privilege
Of loving you in the fall
That when the sky started to grey and the leaves started to live
    on the ground
Instead of in the trees
That I would not only still know you but love you and I would
    say it out loud
And you would say it back
I hoped that I could hold you through the loneliest season
And it wouldn't feel lonely anymore

When I loved you in the fall
All I could do was hope that you would love me through the winter
When it was too cold outside to bear it
Even though enough time will have gone by that we will
    have revealed
Some of the secrets of our past
Our habits and idiosyncrasies
Even while the hurt that other people inflicted upon us
    before we met
Was blatantly thawing out
Funny how hurt tends to do that in the colder months while
    everything else stays frozen

When we were in love all through the winter
All I could do was hope we would still be in love in the spring
That as days got longer you wouldn't want to spend your extra time
With anybody other than me

That while everything became new again
You wouldn't feel the pull to start over with somebody else
That the same love that carried us through the other seasons
Would carry us back into the one we started in

But summer comes again and again and again
And we remain as in love as we were
In all the seasons that came before
And the hope that you will continue to choose me has dwindled
Because you only hope for things you can't be sure of yet
My only hope now is that there will be enough seasons
For us to feel like we have adequate time
And I don't think that when you find someone you are willing to
    spend every season with
Until the seasons run out
You ever feel like there is enough time

I met you in the summer
And all I will do now is love you until there aren't any summers left

Being in love is boring

In the way that you get bored as a passenger on road trips

But can happily drift off to sleep knowing you're in good hands

Boring like a movie you've seen a hundred times but still choose to
watch it anyway

Because you love seeing it unfold, even though you know it line by line

Boring like the outfit you feel the most comfortable in

Like the meal you make every week because you love it

Like the story you're being told for the second time

But you have no problem pretending it's the first time you're hearing it

Being in love is boring like watching the sun set every evening

Or noticing that there's a full moon in the sky

Or your go-to coffee order

You've experienced it before

You felt it yesterday and you'll feel it tomorrow

It's not always grandiose and brand-new

But that doesn't mean you don't look forward to its sameness

And sure, it can be repetitive and monotonous

But it's also invulnerable and secure and familiar

Being in love is boring in the best way

I would happily spend the rest of my life being bored

As long as it is with you

I love knowing you
But remember the first day we met
We were so anxious and unsure
When we didn't know yet that we would know each other like this
I miss that a little

I love loving you
So much that it makes me miss the falling part that got us to where
    we are now
I want to take that trip one more time
With you, of course

I love kissing you
But remember the first time we kissed
It actually kind of felt like it wasn't the first time, somehow

I love having dinner with you every night
But remember when we first started cooking for each other
The tender conversations and the little apologies
And the nervous kitchen shuffle around each other
While trying to take turns talking like we would never run out of
    things to say
And we haven't; I hope we never do
But I miss the discomfort that led us to all the relief we have now

Remember when we would meet up for drinks at a restaurant
Before we knew for sure that the seat across from me would
    always be yours
And the one across from you always mine

I would scan the room and find your eyes and walk over to you
In a small but excited way
And I love the big, overexaggerated way that I run to you now
But I can't help but miss the old us, because it brought us here
A train that I would like to stay on forever
Because I know the destination is a place of such beauty
But getting on was so exciting

And now we've got routines
With spontaneity and excitement mixed in where they fit
But just like the first day at a new job
The first night in a new place
The first drive in your new car
Or the first time you fall in love
I love knowing you

But I'd give it all to do it once more, from the start

Being loved by you makes me love me more
I always thought I needed someone to love me
To make up for all the love I wasn't capable of giving myself
But it turns out your love was just a flashlight in a dark room
A candle while the power is out
Or, in my case, a lighthouse in a storm that seems like it might never end
Your love made me realize how worthy I am of all of it
How grateful I am to have finally found it
But also that things weren't so bad before you came along, either
You see, I spent a lot of time with myself before I fell in love with you
I went for long walks and even longer drives with myself
I had long talks, both in mirrors and in my head, with myself
I watched funny movies and laughed with myself
And I cried with myself, too
Oh, did I ever cry
I picked myself up off of floors
And talked myself off of ledges
And, looking back now, I realize how much I had to love myself
To carry myself through all of it
And find my way to you
And now, being loved by you feels like an added bonus
Like a cherry on top
Like a light in the dark
Like everything has always been okay, *but now it's better*
And I see it like that now because of you

To be in love is one thing
To be in love with you
Well, that is another thing entirely
It feels like driving too fast, but on a Sunday morning
Like drinking tea that has gone cold, but only because you talked for so long
Like finishing the best book you've ever read, for the second time
You're not lost and empty when you close it
You're just an expert about that particular plot now
It feels like waking up in the middle of the night, but having hours
    left to sleep
Like forgetting what you're going to say, and then remembering
Like jumping into freezing-cold water, but adapting right away so
    it's entirely enjoyable
It's like someone interrupting you, but with good news
Like running low on gas but knowing you have just enough to get
    where you're going
Being in love with you is like a solution to every conflicting feeling
    I've ever had
Like an up and a down that are so exact, I'm floating
I can't even call it otherworldly because I'm not lost or somewhere new
Loving you feels like sitting in the living room while it snows
Like I could be anywhere, doing anything
But right now, I want to be here

You made me a lover girl again
A changing the sad songs for happy ones
Buying pastel-colored clothing
Getting a full night's sleep because I'm not worried anymore
   kind of lover girl
I wasn't sure I'd ever be a smiling at my phone
Securely attached
Looking at diamond rings on Pinterest
Holding hands on the street
Taking the long way to work
But the short way home to you *kind of lover girl*
I thought you only got to feel it once
And then it fades
But it turns out it comes back way louder than before
And so does the way I laugh
And the way I sing along to songs in the car
And the way I love everyone and you
And myself
It's all louder and brighter now
The way it would be for a lover girl
A girl I didn't think I was anymore
And I had grown to love not being defined
By being a girl who is in love
I woke up from a heartbroken fever dream
And found it fun to sleep in the center of the bed
And empowering to carry in all the groceries in one try by myself
I found joy in looking good for my own gaze
Rather than the male one
I fell in love with dinner for one

ROMANTIC LOVE — 15

And a glass of white wine with a girly show someone else
    would've hated
I found the independence exciting
So exciting, in fact, that I wasn't sure I would ever have room
    for two again
Or enough love to give anyone other than myself
But you made me a lover girl again
Creating a beautiful middle ground where I don't relinquish control
But share it
And I know I can do anything on my own, and I can if I want to
But I don't have to
And I truly think you can only *really* be a lover girl
An all in, fully immersed, completely in love, pulling two wine
    glasses
Out of the cupboard *kind of lover girl*

Because you spent so much time filling only yours

So now that I think about it
Did you make me a lover girl again, or did I?

We need a fairy tale where Prince Charming is a guy
Who always fills up your water bottle when it's empty
And asks how your day was and really listens when you reply
He shows up with takeout from your favorite spot
So you don't have to worry about dinner
A storyline where Prince Charming is patient even though you're
    running late *again*
Because you couldn't decide what to wear
He randomly holds your hand while you're watching TV
He loves your friends wholeheartedly
He doesn't leave you wondering, ever
Where's the fairy tale about a Prince Charming who answers
    your texts
And always says good night
And fiercely loves you for who you are?
He changes where change is needed, and so do you
Because he knows what it means to compromise
Prince Charming needs to be portrayed as the guy
Who makes you feel so deeply comfortable
Being exactly you, with no edits
No ball gown, no dragons
And yes, he's rescuing you, *but he doesn't realize it in the way
    that you do*
Prince Charming needs to be written as a guy like that
Not just happy and in love after all that hardship and fighting
Just happy and in love because you both deserved it all along
A guy who brings flowers when he's *not* sorry

And texts your parents back
And always says good night
And he doesn't wear shining armor, *but you don't either anymore*
And it's because Prince Charming does exist
It's just not in the way you expected
It's even better

But at least you had fun with the *wrong* ones
At least you danced and laughed and drank wine
And swayed down the street holding hands at night
At least it made you dream of what was to come
At least you had fun with them
Even while you wildly miscalculated what it actually was
At the very least you laughed and got to know someone
You got to get butterflies as you walked toward the restaurant
You got to kiss a stranger and experience lust and desire and
    excitement
At least, for a moment, it was fun
At the very least, you get to look back and remember all that
    living you did
The potential in every single person who wound up being the
    wrong one
You will forever watch montages in your head of all those
    first kisses
Until you have your *last* one

You have to have fun with the wrong ones before you find
    the right one

To be with you is to be entirely me
The exact way I would be if no one were watching
Except you're there, too
I am me and I am loved *because* of it
To be with you is to be me but with less pressure
Because you are there to bear the other side of the weight that
    life has to offer
It romanticizes the simple things I love to live for
Like changing leaves and snowstorms and watching TV at night
And makes me somehow love them more
Because I exist with you while it happens all around us
To be with you is exactly where I want to be
Exactly as I am, exactly as you are

I don't know who needs to hear this but:

Find a partner who treats you well

It truly is that simple

And I know it seems obvious, but sometimes it can get lost on you
When there are a million things to be looking for
But being treated well should *never* be negotiable
Because there is a difference between *what you'd like to have*
And what you deserve

You deserve a partner who treats you well

Because in the end
When the music you both like gets harder to hear
And the jokes you both enjoy get harder to remember
When the trips you loved to go on get harder to take
And life gets harder to live with the same ease that you're used to
If you choose a partner who treats you well
You will be left with so much, even as things start to go away
You will be left with kindness and warmth
Respect and generosity
Comfort and tenderness
You will be left with love

The things that will be the very last to go

All you will have is the person your person *really* is and
always has been

And that is why you need a partner who treats you well

It truly is that simple

I want to have coffee with you on Sundays

I want to have coffee while I talk *about* you on Tuesdays at ten a.m.

I want to not have time to get a coffee because you did something
annoying

And I had to deal with it before I left the house

I want to have my coffee go cold because we got distracted

I want to run out of coffee and send you to the store while it snows
to get more

I want to remember the times we went for coffee at the beginning

And how awkwardly we'd place our order, standing in line, not quite
touching

And fight over who would hand over their card first

I want to have a coffee that your mom pours after dinner at your
parents' house

I want to say "We're giving up coffee right now"

While we go on some weird health cleanse together that doesn't work

I want to find little coffee shops while we're on trips to places we've
never been

And both take a sip and nod at each other in approval

As if either of us knows anything about coffee

I want to know your coffee order and surprise you with it

I also want to have coffee that has nothing to do with you

But the smell of the hot drink in my hand still kind of always
reminds me of you

And of all the *insignificant* but *so significant* coffees that are to come

LOST LOVE

or, The Ones Who Went Away but Didn't Break Us

I don't even know if we can call it lost love, can we?

The love was there and now it's gone

When something is lost it is still out there to be found again

And our love left; we couldn't find it if we tried

And we really tried

There is proof all around that it was there in the first place

And love can exist and then leave for good

But I don't know if it still counts as *lost* love

If it completely disappeared

And no one is looking for it anymore

But I wonder sometimes if it actually isn't gone, just lost forever

Still existing somewhere quietly

Knowing how important it is that no one finds it

Tucked away in the back of a sock drawer

Or in the trunk of a car I sold online

Pushed to the back of the pantry like a treat I hid and
    forgot about

Once good, but slowly perishing

Only to be found one day when the "best before" date is
    laughed about

"Can you believe how long this has been sitting in here?"

I will say when I find it

But if our love is just lost forever and not truly gone

If it didn't disappear into thin air the way it seemed to

And is just tucked around a corner somewhere

I do hope that if I ever come across it, I'm able to throw it away
    for good

And not wonder how long it has been sitting there
Out of sight and out of mind

A game of hide-and-seek I stopped playing forever ago

When we were together, I didn't know it would end
So I didn't know I would feel sick to my stomach when the
  guy beside me
At the gym happened to be wearing the same cologne that you
  used to wear
I wonder if I would even notice that he smells exactly like you
If it didn't make me miss you to my core

When we were together, I didn't know it would end
So I could walk through the grocery store down any aisle I wanted
Without feeling weak with sadness, pressed up against the
  shopping cart
Fighting tears at the register thinking of us playfully bumping into
  each other
While we watched the ingredients we were going to cook together
Get rung up one by one
But now it has me swallowing hard while I shake my head no
  to a receipt
And walk out of the store alone

When we were together, I didn't know it would end
So I didn't know I would have to look for you in the driver's seat
Of every car that looks like yours
At every red light and on every freeway
Hoping it was you so I could catch a quick glimpse
To *see* how you're doing
Without having to break my daily resolution to myself
That I won't check your Instagram anymore to *see* how you're doing

When we were together, I didn't know it would end
So I never thought about the little things that would be
    constant reminders
That the end does come
It did come
It's already over
And now my toothbrush is sitting alone where yours once
    kept it company
And there is extra space in the closet
And I'm parking in the middle of the driveway
And I'm sleeping in the middle of the bed

And now, looking at Christmas lights
The first few notes of that song we loved
Reruns of our favorite show to watch together
That guy's cologne at the gym
The car you drove
Certain parts of the grocery store

All of it

All of it reminds me that it ended
And when we were together, I didn't know it would end
I didn't know that all the little things we did would become
    unbearable
Once you were gone

I would've been more careful to pay less attention

We came so close, didn't we
We were almost it
And in some universe, I like to believe that we were
Even though in this one we just didn't fit
And it wasn't a square-and-circle kind of mismatch
It was far less obvious than that
The kind where we tried to jam the pieces together again and again
Not sure exactly why they just wouldn't attach properly

We came so close we probably could've tried forever
And wound up living a life where we both wondered what would've
    happened
If we didn't end up together
Because it would seem to us both that there *must* be more out there
    than this
But it would be too late, and we'd have both settled for mediocrity
Settled for almost fitting

And we would've let subpar be the norm
We would've gotten married, and we would've had kids
And they would love us
But quietly hope for a different kind of love when they grow up
Than the kind that their parents have for each other

One that's a little larger, one that fits a little better

And there is something so heartbreaking about the one you *almost*
    made it with

You and I almost made it

And I think the most heartbreaking thing of all would be if we had

The person who ruined you because they didn't love you properly
Probably isn't going to ruin the next person in the same way
They may actually never do it again
And I know it's hard not to sit in the front row and expect it to happen
In the same way that you're certain the train you're waiting for will show
Or the alarm you set will go off in the morning
You can expect it, but you can't be sure
And you're not evil to hope the pattern repeats itself
So you can have more proof that it was *them* and not *you*
It doesn't make you a bad person to look at photos of their new person
    on Instagram
And try to pinpoint whether or not the light in their eyes is fading as
    time passes
The same way that it did in yours
It's not strange to lie awake at night and wonder if they're fighting
    all the time
Or if the person they chose after you feels like they're begging for
    affection like you did
But it's important to remember not to spend your time pitying them,
    either

Because there is a chance that the person who ruined you
Is making someone else the happiest person in the world

And sometimes it's not even a matter of people changing or growing
    or maturing
It's a matter of being right for each other or not
And one of the most deeply heartbreaking parts of being alive
Is that some unlucky people are capable of loving the *wrong* person

As much as they will love the *right* person
And some people are lucky because they aren't capable of that
And in this way, you are one of the unlucky ones
You are someone who can love the wrong person so fiercely
That you will spend forever thinking they must be incapable of love
Because they didn't love the wrong person, too
They didn't love you

And the idea that the person who ruined you won't ruin the next
    person
Is one of the most ambivalent feelings you will ever get to know
Because you want them to be happy
But not as badly as you want you to be happy
And as sure as the sun will rise (something you can be certain of)
Proper love goes in both directions
And soulmates love *each other*
And sometimes being ruined by someone is the best thing
    that could have happened
Because it's always a beginning disguised as an ending
And you get to realize how much you're capable of feeling
And you will chase that emotion forever and ever
Until you find it with someone who has probably ruined
    someone else
But they wouldn't ever dream of ruining you

———————

"I used to be like in love with him"
I say to my friends over wine at the table
Through a laugh when his name comes up
Like it doesn't matter; like it never did
It's funny the words we choose to describe the way we *used* to feel
So I say "I used to be like in love with him"
Instead of
"I used to revolve around him"
"I used to obsess over him"
"I used to cry myself to sleep about him"
"I used to drink wine just like this to try to not be so
Overwhelmingly overtaken by the thought of him"
"I used to wait around for him"
"I used to think that I could change him"
"I used to be in love with him"
Not *like* in love, *in love*
And I think that everything that once made you cry
Is allowed to make you laugh afterward
So I do; I laugh
But there was nothing funny about it
And now when I bring you up, everyone erupts
Because they all remember the shell of the person I was
When I was *like* in love
And they remember unanswered texts and an empty seat at the table
And I remember an empty pit in my stomach while I waited to have
    my worth decided
By a late-night invitation
And I don't really know what he would remember but I can only
    assume

It's something along the lines of
"*Oh, her—she was like in love with me*"
And he'd be right; I was
But being in love with him
Was never something I liked
It was just something that happened

What about the relationship that ended with a reciprocal "I will
    always love you"
And you both meant it
You just couldn't figure out for the life of either of you how to make
    it work
You were both so in love, *but it had to end*
And there are not many things in life more confusing than a *shift* in love
From romantic to just the way you love anyone else
It's not a tie that can be severed easily
And it's not a moment that can be pinpointed
There is not one day that the shift happens
But I think it's important to remember that not all relationships end
Because there is no love there
There are just so many different types of love
And not all can breathe air into romance
You can have goodbye on your lips and love in your heart
    simultaneously
You don't have to leave every relationship with a horrific story
To tell your friends once it's over
And I don't know if the relationship ending with a reciprocal "I will
    always love you"
Makes it easier or harder
Because confusion can hurt just as much as anger
And no contact with someone you want nothing to do with
Is a lot easier than with someone you will always love
Because the love you are feeling doesn't necessarily breathe air into
    friendship, either
Sometimes you just have to keep breathing, separately
And keep loving, quietly

And walk away, peacefully
With a tiny little piece of your heart never being fully vacant
Because love lived there once, and it's okay if it always does
You can unlearn a lesson, but you never forget one
And next time you will love bigger and better
And you will know that even though it *was* love
It was the wrong kind
Because you gave yourselves the freedom to find the right one

Nothing was ever going to be okay again
And then it was
I was never going to stop crying over you
And then I did
It was going to rain forever
And then it was sunny
I was never going to leave the house
And then I was laughing around a table at a happy hour with friends
I was never going to want anyone else
And then I was kissing a stranger on a dance floor
I was never going to trust someone again
And then I was telling someone my deepest secrets in the middle
   of the night
I was going to give up on love
And then I realized it was all around me the whole time
When you were there, and when you weren't, too
I was never going to be able to survive it
And then I lived through it in such big ways
That I'm almost happy it happened
I didn't have faith in me to exist without you
And then I realized how wrong I was to think that
And I know now, this is just how life works
And in the same way that nothing was ever going to be okay again
And then it was
Everything will be okay again
And then it won't
And then it will be again after that

Somehow getting through the loss of you means I can get through
anything once
And then I can do it again and again and again

I loved you so much that the day you left me
I begged you for five more minutes
I know it sounds sad but I kind of miss being someone
Who is capable of loving that much
I truly think you only get to do it once
I think we all only have it in us to beg one person to stay
And after that you shed your skin for a harder shell
And you never beg anyone to love you ever again
Sure, you might implore or ask a few too many times
But you will never beg for five more minutes
That's the one heartbreak you swear you won't survive
And then you surprise yourself when you do
And you come out of it a different person
A person who survives stuff; who knew?
And now the only thing you could never live through again
Is a person who makes you beg for them
I still remember the feeling of that kind of love
The way you remember all the words when an old song starts to play
And in the same way that song got overplayed and everyone grew
    tired of it
I grew tired of feeling so deeply
And I will never beg for five more minutes from anyone
Who is choosing to leave me
Ever again

The quiet that came after I accepted the loss of you
Wasn't deafening
It was just quiet
It felt like springtime
Everything was new and you were not mine anymore
And that was okay
It was the kind of quiet where you can hear kids playing in the
    distance
The occasional dog barking
Wind blowing through trees
Cars driving by
Wind chimes and quiet banter as people walk past
The world moving on, and me, too
It was the kind of quiet that you need when you're looking for
    a parking spot
Or turning onto your street
Just a slight hum in the background right as you make it to your
    destination
Not a deafening quiet, just quiet

The kind I haven't felt in a long, long time

Wanting it to be you
Felt like wanting things as a kid
Begging for them on my knees
And feeling so helpless when the answer was no
Because there was nothing I could do
And I didn't have the emotional maturity to understand that
    I had to accept it
I could not wrap my head around it
I wanted it to be you so badly
And it felt like having a toy ripped out of my hands at the store
Before we could pass through the exit
I couldn't imagine another way after picturing how good it would be
If I could just have that one thing I wanted
And in those moments, I lost all sense of civility
Kicking and screaming
Wanting and needing
Head sore from crying and heaving
Rejection therapy at its finest
Wanting it to be you when it couldn't felt like that
And only later did I realize I didn't need that toy
Like I didn't need you
But for some reason I can't remember exactly which item it was
I had to let go of at the till
But I remember everything about the person who wouldn't let me
    have them
That toy didn't become a part of my identity
But me not getting to have you did
And I know now that anything you have to beg for was never yours
    to begin with

And I know there is no such thing as "can't live without"
Because I have continued living each and every time
And I now know the difference between *wanting* and *needing*
I didn't ever *need* any of the things I kicked and screamed for
But my God did I ever want them

If you're not the one they want, it's not their loss
And it's not yours, either
It's the first thing your friends say while you're crying into a
    vodka soda
About someone who doesn't love you back
Someone who will never love you the way that you love them
"It's their loss"

It's not their loss
But it is also not yours

Because you deserve to be loved by someone *who loves you*
In the big, heavy, all-encompassing way that you have loved people
Who don't feel the same
And they deserve to love someone like that, too
So if they don't love you properly, to lose you is not their loss
And to lose them is entirely your gain
Because a true loss is being settled for
And, in return, them settling
To fight for reciprocal love until you are blue in the face would be the
    ultimate shortfall
From someone who would have loved *like you* if given the chance
To give it away to someone *other* than you
The true definition of a loss for both of you
Things can hurt and still be for the best
And you are allowed to grieve love that you gave and did not receive
    in return
Because it feels like one of life's greatest losses

But something can only be a loss if you label it as one
If they didn't want you, losing you was not their loss

And it definitely wasn't yours, either

It can still be love even if it doesn't last forever
And it was love; I stand firm in that
I loved you

It can still be love even if you're glad it ended
And I am glad; I'm sure of that
But I loved you

It can still be love even if it doesn't leave you heaving when it
    goes away
I did not miss a single breath
And I loved you

It was still love even if you don't feel the need to lie and say it wasn't
Just because it drew to a close
I would tell anyone that I loved you

When I am asked if I've been in love more than once
I will always say yes with a smile on my face and think of you
Because I loved you

And I can only do this because I don't love you anymore

But I did

When you think about me, what does it feel like
Does it happen upon you, or does it happen to you
Does it make you wish I never happened, or glad I did
Do you feel the thought of me in your stomach or in your chest
Do you miss me in a way that makes you feel sick
Or a way that makes you smile a little while you're alone in your car
When you think about me, does it feel like remembering a word you
    forgot
Or a scene from a movie you wish you had never seen in the first place
Does it feel like riding down a hill with your feet off the pedals
Or does it feel like falling off your bike onto cement
When I cross your mind, is it like November or June
Is it cold air and grey skies and wet sidewalks
Or a hot day and a cold drink and the momentary feeling that life
    is kind
I know how I feel when you cross my mind
I know it so intimately because I spend so much time with the
    thought of you
I've memorized the way it takes over my body
You creep into my head through a door I've been meaning to change
    the locks to
But haven't gotten around to it
I'm sure I will eventually
And as much as I'm sure you'd like it not to be the case
I've still got the keys to your door, too
I don't mean to visit, but somehow I always end up driving down
    your street
And finding my way in, though the visits have gotten shorter and
    shorter

I want to know how it feels when I stop by
Does it happen upon you, or does it happen to you
Does it make you wish I never happened, or glad I did

Grieving the living
Is not normalized in the same way as the grief
That comes to mind when you hear that word
But we grieve the living, and it hurts
All the same and all the time
A grief that creeps up on you when you least expect it
The grieving of the relationship that could've been
With the person who could've been there, but isn't
And what makes it worse is that when you grieve the living
You not only have to find the strength to go on without them
You have to find the strength to keep it that way
Because you have to restrain yourself from going back
From stitching together the tie that you severed because you
    needed to
From drawing dotted lines on maps to find a person
Who doesn't want to be found

Grieving the living is a grief that one of you has chosen
And that makes it unbearable
But it also makes you feel like you are not allowed to be filled with
    sadness
Or anguish or heartache because they're not dead, they're only
    dead to you
But you are
You are entirely entitled to the gnawing, aching, undefeatable grief
That people feel with the absence of a person who, if things had
    been different
Goodbye may not have been the only choice

Your grief for the living is still grief
It still counts
It will always hurt
Because that is what grief was made to do

Watching someone you're in love with fall in love with someone else
Is a feeling unlike any other
It's hopeless in a way you can only understand if you have felt it
    yourself
Because you so desperately want something you cannot have, no
    matter what you do
And you can change everything about yourself
The clothes you wear, the things you say
The jokes you laugh at, the bars you go to
But no matter what you change
You can't change their mind

You want so terribly to be wanted
So you lie in bed at night and you picture them with someone else
And you feel it in the deepest parts of you
Parts you didn't know existed
And no matter how hard you try
Or how happy you are
Or how far you've moved on
You never forget the feeling of not being wanted by someone you
    wanted
And you especially never forget the feeling of the person you wanted
Wanting someone else

You don't even *know* them and you wish you *were* them
Because you are grief-stricken by the *maybe* that has turned into
    a definite *no*
The uncertainty that always was
Is now a certainty, and it is far from in your favor

They have found what they were looking for in someone other than you

So you hopelessly watch
And even if all the old wives' tales are true
And this really *is* for the better
And the person who is meant for you will want you back
And your time will come, and your love is out there
It all sounds promising, but it hurts all the same

Not being wanted by the person you wanted stays with you forever
And you will feel better eventually, but you will never forget the way
    it felt
A fundamental piece of your character
An unavoidable part of being human

Wanting to be wanted, and not getting what you want

I thought we were soulmates
You didn't, but I did
I thought we would be so in love if you ever came around
You didn't love me yet, but you would
You were about to change your mind
You were about to fall in love with me
Every day I waited was another chance for you to reconsider
Because being considered by you felt like the highest form of flattery
While being loved by me meant nothing to you
Although I think it's human nature to want to be wanted, so I think you
    didn't mind that part
And I had myself convinced it would be your loss, somehow
If the girl you didn't want walked away from you
And that walking away would be my loss, too
Because then I would lose you

But I never had you; you had me

And in the moment it felt like a math equation I couldn't get right
No matter how many times I tried
I could not understand that we cannot be soulmates if it's one-sided
If I want you and you *don't* want me, then this isn't meant to be, and
    you are not the one
I hoped so deeply that the curtains would open, or the clouds would
    clear
And it would be sunny everywhere all the time
And you would love me, too
As if it wouldn't be heavy on my shoulders forever that the only way
    to have you

Was to persuade you
To exhaust all resources and wear out all your options
And you would settle for me, and we would be soulmates

But soulmates don't *settle* for each other
Even though in the moment, I would've done anything to have you
   settle for me

And it turns out that time was the answer
And the curtains did open
And the clouds did clear

And we weren't soulmates after all

But for a moment, I really thought we were

I know that we don't know each other anymore
But that doesn't mean I don't hope you get home safe
Even if I don't know exactly where home is for you these days
I know we don't know each other anymore
But that doesn't mean I don't want you to get a good sleep each night
    when you close your eyes
Or that I hope you don't get tickets when your favorite band comes
    to town
Or that I don't hope you finally got rid of those shoes and treated
    yourself to some new ones
We don't know each other anymore
But I hope you still enjoy the kind of peace and quiet that I couldn't
    provide you
And I hope you found it in someone you love getting to know more
    each day
I hope you landed in the life you wanted, even though it was so
    different from the one I did
Just because I don't know you anymore
Doesn't mean I wish I never got to
It doesn't mean I wish I never loved you
It also doesn't mean I wish this went any other way

I don't wish it didn't end

But it is because I knew you
That I hope you've had roundtable talks with your demons in the
    same way I have
And that you've reconciled with most of them
And that I am not one of yours, because you are not one of mine

Because I knew you
I know how happy you will make someone who isn't anything
   like me
And I think all along we both knew that a day would come
When we didn't know each other anymore

And I don't know

I don't know how your day was yesterday or how it will go today
   or tomorrow
I don't know how well you sleep at night
I don't know what song is your favorite right now
I don't know how your parents are doing
And I don't know if you still drive that car with the crank windows
And the loud beeps when you refuse to buckle up for short drives

And I know I don't know you anymore

But I still hope you wear your seat belt

FAMILY LOVE

or, The Ones We Were Given

I'm always lucky because *you* are my mom
I could buy a million lottery tickets and never win a dime
Step on every crack in every sidewalk
Break mirrors, walk under ladders
And open umbrellas indoors each day
And I would still be lucky
I could stand on street corners on rainy days
While cars splash through puddles and ruin my favorite jeans
I could never pass another piece of wood to knock on
And see only black cats cross my path
I could shrink all my best wool sweaters in the dryer
And because you are my mom, none of it would matter
I would still be the luckiest person there ever was
Because you overrule the bad stuff
Calling you my mom is like the number seven
It's like all the dream catchers and rabbits' feet
And ladybugs and lucky pennies combined
And because of that, I will always be lucky
I know that, since we've always made our luck from scratch
And we never won a single lottery in the literal sense
But we've always been rich in our own ways
I know because you held my hand as I stepped on every crack in the
        sidewalk by accident
Without ever wincing once
You cleaned up broken glass and climbed ladders like you were
        Santa Claus
And I always had an umbrella,
Even though I never remembered to bring them home from school
You supplied them endlessly

On days when it felt like the rain might never stop falling
Or when the only wood we had to knock on was from Ikea
And we built it ourselves
Because you're my mom, there was always another clean sweater
   in the drawer
Even when my favorite got shrunk in the dryer
I have always been lucky
And I always will be lucky
Because you're my mom

There are two labels when it comes to families
Conventional and unconventional
Where the criteria have a lot to do with
Two parents who stay together
Multiple siblings
A clean, well-decorated house
Math homework at the kitchen table
A minivan with sliding doors
Maybe a fence around the backyard, white picket or not
A little disposable income to take a vacation each year
Pizza on Friday nights
A family that upholds common and widely accepted values
The dictionary definition of a conventional family
Rarely has much to do with the love that exists there
Always described as the way it's supposed to *look*
Rather than the way it's supposed to *feel*
The labels of conventional and unconventional when it comes
    to family
Will never make sense to me
Because a conventional family should be described as
A place where love lives unconditionally
Where people choose one another
And forgive one another
Where the floors aren't always made of eggshells
A conventional family should be defined as "home"
The feeling, not the place
And yes, they're basically the same word with the difference
    of two letters
But being labeled as an unconventional family

Sometimes leaves you feeling like something is missing
Like you're on the wrong side of the train tracks
Or living on the outskirts
Like there's something to be jealous of
But there's not
Because to be unconventional means to *go against*
But if anything, it's the opposite
It's making something that feels like home out of something that
    might not have
You fought for it, not against it

I know one of these days I'm going to regret moving far away
And it'll be an inevitable and deeply painful regret
That I would feel anyway no matter what I chose
Because I think as life goes on
You are bound to feel grief, and it will always be associated
    with regret
Wishing you spent more time with the people you love
All the birthdays I didn't come home for
And the Christmases I said I would never dare to miss
But I've missed a few now, haven't I?
I'm going to regret this distance, I will

I already do

It's heavy in my throat when I leave my childhood room to head
    to the airport
And it's in the pit of my stomach when I sit across from my high
    school friends
And realize that we are all adults now
And the way life has changed us between this visit and the last one
Is far more obvious than it would be
If I were around more often, *but I'm not*

So now I face the cold, lonely moments before I fall asleep at night
When I picture the life and friends and family I left behind
And I know exactly where the emptiness comes from
I know exactly the source of the regret
But had I stayed I worry I would feel something was missing
And I'd never have figured out what it was

And in ways I've won, because I call two places home
But in ways I've lost, because I cannot be in both of them at once

It's hard to not always feel like a part of you is missing, no matter
    where you are
Being far away
The ultimate sacrifice, as well as the ultimate journey
And I will call with the bad news that I will not be home for
    Christmas this year once again
But in turn I am now able to be home for Christmas
It'll just be this home instead of that one

And in my head, it will never feel right or make sense
But it'll be the way it is

If you've ever had a dog, you know
You know what it's like to be loved just for being exactly who you are
You could have nothing and you'd still be everything to them
You could lose it all and they wouldn't bat an eye
In the unconditional way you can only understand
If you've ever had a dog
You know how to find the good in a slow walk in the rain, even while
you're chilled to the bone
You know that even on the worst day ever, there's a little happiness on
the other side of the door, if only for a moment
You know how to selflessly surrender your last and best bite of food
without ever hearing a thank-you
But you have felt the thank-yous endlessly
If you've ever had a dog
You've been a protector and been protected
You've been viewed as everything, even in moments when you've had
nothing left to give
Because in a world where you have a dog
Just putting your feet on the ground in the morning
Is enough to be cheered on endlessly
And if that's not the kind of unwavering love you need to feel like
you're enough
I don't know what is
And if you've ever had a dog, you know
That the love is unconditional
But the time you get is not
And years are fast, but dog years are faster
If you've ever had a dog, you will know
One of the greatest loves

And one of the greatest heartbreaks
Is having a dog
But you will carry the feeling of being loved
Just for being who you are
Until the end of time
You will always know in some way or another
That you are enough
And it will be because you had a dog

I fear that one day I will have a daughter
Who cries about her broken heart
And when I try to console her
She will tell me that I could never understand
That I've never felt like that before
That there's no way I could possibly relate
And she will slam her door in my face
And I will stand on the other side of it
And for a moment I will think of *you*
Because I think heartbreaks like that never stop crossing your mind

Even when you are older

Even when you're somebody's mom

And we're born to think our moms are *just moms*
And that's all they've ever been
They've never had their hearts broken by someone who made them
    not leave their bedroom for days on end
My daughter will think that I'm just her mom

I know nothing and everything all at once
And I've never felt the constant and all-encompassing ache that
    comes with something ending
That you don't want to end

So I will stand on the other side of her door
Right after she slams it in my face
And we will cry in unison

Because she thinks that I will never understand
And I remember so vividly how deeply I understand
And she is heartbroken
And I am, too, because she is part of me

And I know exactly how she feels

One day she will understand

If I could see you one more time
I know just what I'd do
Cause all I've thought of since you left
Is one more day with you

There are notes in every margin
About everything you've missed
And with every passing day
More gets added to the list

I'd probably invite you
To do things simple and mundane
Like walk to get a coffee
Or listen to the rain

I'd talk about tomorrow
Like I know it's going to come
And for a few brief moments
Everything would not feel numb

I'd let you speak forever
And hear every word you say
I won't take it for granted
Since I know you go away

I'd ask you all the questions
That I wish I'd asked before
I'd tell you that without you
I am not whole anymore

I'd make sure that before you leave again
You know the truth
About the very depths of the amount
That I love you

Before we said goodbye
I would hold you tight as ever
The way you hold somebody
Right before they leave forever

I'd say I'll think of you
Every part of every day
And you'd tell me it won't be life
If I live it that way

That you will be a part
Of everything I ever am
That I need to move on
Instead of trying to understand

And as our time ran out again
I'd try to act real tough
But no amount of time with you
Could ever be enough

But I won't see you just once more
But again and again and again
Because the day that I do not
Will mean I've found my end

And even when that day does come
I'll see you that day, too
Cause the first person I'm looking for
Once I get there
Is you

"Broken home" sounds awful
But it isn't really
Not every time, anyway
I think as kids in the same way we believe in Prince Charming
And magic and Santa
We believe in parents who never break up
And when they do we think it's a mess and everything's shattered
And it's our fault
When a lot of the time it's just the first step toward freedom
From a relationship that wasn't meant to be

But when we're little we don't see our parents as two adults
Who fell in love and then fell out of it
We see them as two people who have to be living under one roof
Or they're doing it all wrong
It might be one of life's most profound misfortunes
That it takes a young mind so long to comprehend
Why love goes away
And why homes get broken in the first place
And often they're only broken in the way that your car breaks down
Because they truly have been through too much

And it's stressful but the new one feels so right once it's yours
It's broken in a way that you split a granola bar in half to feed two
    hungry people
And neither is full right now, *but at least nobody is starving anymore*
Broken like a Christmas ornament that meant a lot to you
Devastating in the moment, but Christmas will go on

And for me a broken home felt like the worst thing
At the same time that it was the best thing for the people who
loved me the most
Everything isn't as it seems all the time
And it turns out that broken isn't always bad
Especially when there's still a home

I'm a long-distance daughter
But I haven't always been
I used to wake up in the middle of the night
And walk not ten steps
Before I was tucked into my mother's bed
Pressed up beside her
Nothing bad could happen there
No, it never could
And it never did
I'm a long-distance daughter
But I haven't always been
I used to get annoyed because there wasn't enough privacy
For me to finish getting ready before my mother would start telling
    me how beautiful I looked
She always needed to know exactly where I was going
Now I have all the space in the world
Before she sees the posts online
And tells me how beautiful I look in the photos
"When did you take that, honey? Why were you all dressed up?
    You looked beautiful"
I'm a long-distance daughter
And now when I wake up in the middle of the night
I lie in the dark
With no other bed to get up and crawl into
Where I'm sure nothing bad will ever happen
And I think about whether or not
Being a long-distance daughter was the right thing to do
Will I regret this forever one day?
Because one day I will be a long-distance daughter

In universes rather than miles
And my mother's voicemail that she never lets me hear
Because she is always so eager to answer the phone
Will be the only thing I get to hear when I call
And that's the thing about being a long-distance daughter
You'll never know if it was the right choice
You'll never feel at ease with the decision to leave
No matter how wonderful the life you created for yourself

You left behind the person who gave you a life to create

I hope you don't miss me in heaven as badly as I miss you here
I hope for you the silence is peaceful
And the thought of me feels like déjà vu
A wave of familiarity that you can't quite put your finger on
Empty for only a moment once in a while
And gone like the wind after that
I hope when you got there, you were swept over by a wave of
	forgetfulness
So you're still entirely full of life and happiness *but you can't
	remember why*
And pieces of me are a part of you in such a way that you feel even
	more complete
I can't imagine heaven feels how I feel without you, and I hope it
	doesn't
I hope you yearn for nothing and no one
I hope there is no pain at all
Maybe I am feeling both of ours at once, and that's why it feels this
	heavy
If that's the case, it means you are with me, and I'm okay with that
I hope that in heaven grief does not exist
And I show up in your dreams on occasion
And the feeling of having me near you lingers with you through
	the morning after you wake up
I hope those are the same nights you show up in mine
And if in heaven you can't remember me at all
I hope the wave of forgetfulness that overtook you when you arrived
Turns into an ocean of remembering when we meet again
Like we never spent a moment apart
And I will forget what it was like to be without you

And you will never have known what it was like to be without me
Because you found the peace I'd hoped you'd find
While I found my way back to you

I would love to meet my parents *before*
Before they knew me, before they knew each other
I would love to know them while life was still simple
Before they had such intense responsibilities
Before there was someone on the planet who believed they had
     all the answers
Before they had to pretend they did
I would love to exist around them as people who weren't held
     accountable
For making my world spin around and around
I would want them to tell me all the things they don't have the
     solutions for
The things they worry about
The way they see their lives panning out
I would ask what their hopes are for their future children
And see if I line up in any way
I'd ask what kind of house they hope to live in in the future
The things they hope to see and do before they settle down
I would want to know what drinks they used to order at the bar
The way they used to take their coffee
How their respective apartments looked when they lived on
     their own
I'd want to know about the people who had already broken their
     hearts
I'd want to meet them for breakfast knowing the first thing they
     thought about that day
Wasn't my well-being
I'd want to drunkenly run into my mom when she was young
     and have her ask me for a lighter

I'd want to see what my dad put into his grocery cart when he
 shopped for only himself in his early twenties
I'd want to soak in the sense of ease that I know doesn't exist in the
 way it did before me
I think one of life's greatest tragedies is never getting to know who
 our parents were
Before us
That we will never get to know them to their core, the way we do
 with old friends
That we'll never get to meet them
And that they probably never even got a chance to say goodbye
Because when it comes to parents
There is a before you and an after you
There was an each of them
A both of them
And an all of us
And they will always say that the part when they got to be our
 parents was the *best* part
But I know there is a past that they grieve that we are not even
 close to being able to imagine
A freedom, a sense of wonder, and the kind of understanding
 and connection
We would only know if we met them *before*

When you're growing up
Your parents love to tell you stories about the things you used to do
"You used to be so small"
"You used to love that toy"
"You used to crawl into bed with me when you had a nightmare"
You never really realize the power of those two words
"Used to"
Or the fear that comes along with the idea that you will use them
    when you talk about your parents one day
"My mom used to make that joke"
"My dad used to love that place"
"My mom used to call every Sunday"
"My dad used to play that song all the time"
The smallest words, with the most meaning
The were, the was, the used to
Because it's the way you describe something that is no longer
Something that only lives on as a memory
Something that *happened*
And in the same way that your parents told the stories of the used-to
With a smile on their face and an ache in the pit of their stomach
You will tell stories about them and the things they *used* to do

It's all just proof that a dog lives here
Teeth marks in the baseboards
Crumpled up mats by the front door
Nothing without fur on it anymore
It's all just proof that a dog lives here

Toes getting stomped on as you take off your shoes
Bundling up for the freezing cold when it's the last thing you
    want to do
Coming home from the party when it feels too soon
It's all just proof that a dog lives here

Shushing every time the doorbell rings
Postponing the purchase of nice new things
The joy that the front door always brings
It's all just proof that a dog lives here

Being loved for every single thing that you are
Constantly needing to vacuum the car
Your regular walk becoming too far
It's all just proof that a dog lives here

The signs of the slowing down never feel good
The patches on their favorite parts of the hardwood
The knowing you'd stop time for them if you could
It's all just proof that a dog lives here

The parts of the house not aesthetically pleasing
The wait by the door when they know that you're leaving

The fear that without them there wouldn't be meaning
It's all just proof that a dog lives here

And the day will come when you can refinish the floors
And get a new couch and repaint the baseboards
But you won't want to anymore
Because it's all just proof that a dog lived here

And I know it can get overwhelmingly messy
But in the grand scheme it is all just a blessing
Because of all the good years your house is getting
All because a dog lives here

We didn't have much money growing up
But I was rich
So rich I didn't know what to do with all my riches
Because we didn't have much money
But I had this bicycle and a side door to run through after I rode it
And an old house that didn't get many upgrades, but my friends
always wanted to come over
We were allowed to jump on the couches because they were falling
apart anyway
We didn't have much money growing up
But I was rich because the secondhand store always had the coolest,
most colorful stuff
And when I outgrew it, my grandma would sew it into quilts or
repurpose it as rags
To wipe down tables after my friends stayed over
And even though we didn't have much money
My mom always used the best breakfast ingredients on those
mornings
The fence that kept the dog in was always breaking, but my mom
knew how to fix it herself
And now I'm really good at fixing things myself, too—
Or at least I'm never scared to try
I was rich in a way that I learned to drive in a seven-seater van
That could fit so many people I love all at once
And I did just that
We didn't have a lot of money, but we had a whole lot of other
things—
Like two-can-dine coupons for dinners that I got to share
with my family

And more people in one hotel room than you'd think possible because
we took the trips anyway, even if the drive was long and the room
was small
We had a warm life and a warm house, even though it was more
stressful for us than for some others if the furnace needed work—
but it always ended up fixed
We weren't rich in the way we always wished
But we were rich in a way that I wish I could have back
And I hope, when I have a family of my own, we are rich, too—and I
think we will be
The kind of rich that gets passed down through generations
The kind where you don't have a lot of money, but there's a lot of love
I grew up rich
And I think it shows

If I have a daughter
And she grows up to be like me
I know she will be just fine
More than fine, actually
I know under no uncertain terms
That she will figure it out, *eventually*
Even if the uncertainty is overwhelming in the lead-up
Which, if she's like me, it will be
If I have a daughter and she grows up to be like me
She will be resilient and steadfast
She will want help but will seldom need it
And I know without a shadow of a doubt
She will be okay
She will give herself a very hard time
Most of the time
Like I do
I know that for sure
Because I question myself in every way
But somehow I know if my daughter is like me
I won't question who she is or what she's capable of
She will always find the answers she's looking for
Even if people continually question the routes she takes to find them
And I really do hope I have a daughter
Who is like me in her own way
Not only so I can make her feel loved for everything she is
But so I can finally love the things about me
I've always had a hard time wrapping my head around
Because nothing about her will be hard for me to love
If I have a daughter and she turns out like me

I will understand her
Even the things I've always misunderstood about myself
And I will see all the right things I'd been mixing up with wrong
    things all this time
So if you're ever struggling with who you are
I advise you to ask yourself how you would feel
If you had a daughter
And she had a mind and a heart like yours
Because I think you'd be extremely proud
And profoundly relieved
To know that she will be just fine

I want to go back to my childhood so badly
And I don't even want to stay forever
I just want to visit
And knowing that no matter what I cannot go back ever again
Creates an ache and a longing that no one will ever have the words for
Even though I will spend my life trying to find them
It feels like standing in a glass house, and I can see it so perfectly
But I have to just watch the memories playing back on the other side
I can feel it, but I can't have it
The way the warm sidewalk felt in the summer on little feet
And the way rocks would get embedded in my knees
While I scraped chalk along the sidewalk
The way bike pedals felt against bare feet
The way the house phone sounded
The way the cool air felt on Halloween night
Before sorting through candy on the living room floor
The sliding van door shutting me into the back seat on Christmas
The smell of microwave popcorn on movie night
The hopeless feeling of being sent to my room
Snowsuits and gloves that were connected by a string through the
    back of my coat
Feeling homesick at sleepovers
Eating spaghetti
The distant sound of the TV down the hall while I was supposed to
    be asleep
I can see it and I can feel it
But I can't have it
And it hurts
Because it's gone, but it's not because it will always live in me

And nothing will ever be the same as it was

But we all only get to do it once

And maybe that's why it means so much

Maybe that's why it hurts so badly

And maybe the aching and the longing of being stuck here and
    wanting to be there

Is the only thing we'll all ever have in common

That's just part of losing someone
Isn't it?
Looking at the chair they used to sit in
And feeling like your insides are getting
Pulled out of you all at once
Christmas always feeling
Good and uneasy simultaneously
Your heart being so close to healing
Like the way you can always feel the part of your body where
    a bone was broken
Even after it's better
It's just not as strong as it used to be
Feeling half empty during your biggest moments
That would've been full *if they had been there*
And wishing you could just enjoy things
While also never wanting them to stop crossing your mind
It's a lifetime of painfully contradictory feelings
And it's all just a part of the process
The motions that every single one of us goes through
Every single one of us, without fail
The jaded, rusty edge of grief
That cuts through the simplest of moments
And it makes you feel
Like the weakest person on earth
All the while saying to yourself
"Well, that's just a part of losing someone, I guess"
In the nonchalant way
That only the strongest person on earth
Would say something like that

The sound of your parents' voices is like

The sound of rain with the window open after a nap

The smell of carrots roasting in the oven

The way it feels when it's just about to snow for the first time but
hasn't yet

The sound of your mother's voice is like

Hand cream on really dry hands

Closing the textbook once you've finished your math homework

A deep breath on a night in August

Your parents' voices sound the way love feels

And if you still have a way to hear the sound of your parents' voices

Do it every chance you get

Because no other parents sound like your parents

TOXIC LOVE

or, The Ones We Never *Really* Get Over

You made me feel like I needed to be a better person
But I *was* the better person
I still am the better person
And I don't know what kind of person you are now
But I hope you've become a better person than you were
Good people don't make good people feel like bad people
They don't convince kind people they're unkind
And compassionate people that they lack empathy
Good people don't take advantage of good people
Or anyone, for that matter
You turned my trust into naivety
You made a strong person weak
And you did it all with your words, so now it is my turn to do it with mine
I am a good person
And good people don't make other people feel bad about themselves
So I will leave the words I want to use to describe you out of this
And tell you the truth about who I actually am
Instead of letting us both believe I am the person you think you reduced me to
I am headstrong and willfully self-assured
I am fiercely loyal, *but you know that already*
I am smart and kind
I am a good person
And of the two of us, I am the bigger person
The stronger person, the freer person

The better person

I am a better person than you

I left the bar to come and see you

I did my makeup and my hair
I bought a new outfit
I wore a perfume I know you like *even though you weren't coming*
I asked the Uber driver to turn on the radio
And danced the whole way there with my friends
I waited in line and I paid the cover and then I thought about you
I tried not to, but I did
I kept checking my phone to see if I'd heard from you
Everyone had fun and I waited for reassurance from you
You aren't mine and I'm not yours
I'm not dictating your night, but you're dictating mine
I want to be the cool girl
The unreachable girl
The girl who doesn't care

But I care *so much*

So as soon as you ask me to
I leave the bar to come and see you
I sit in the Uber in silence; I do not ask him to turn on the radio
I go to your apartment and I look beautiful
And you do not even clear the dishes from the counter or make
    your bed
You don't tell me I look good; *you just touch me like I do*
You don't ask me how my night was because you know it was all
    about you

It always is

And I left the bar for you

While I let my bar fall far too low
So low I cannot ever go lower

So I guess it's only up from here, right?

I wish I'd never met you
I don't think there was any good reason behind it
I think it was an accident
Like fate got distracted looking at its phone
And when it looked back up
We had crashed into each other
And it was too late

The damage was done and we had met

I don't think it was a good lesson
Or that it made me tough
Or a better person
I think it just became a part of the reason I'm not the same anymore
The reason I'm so closed off
The reason I do not trust people the way I used to

I don't think we were supposed to meet
I think it was a total misfortune
And sometimes I think about the day it happened
And how one minor decision
Could have stopped the whole thing
One moment could've saved me years
Because if we had never met
I would still be all the good parts of me
And there would be fewer parts
That need to be fixed

And I would still go for drives

But you would not enter my thoughts
Like you're robbing a bank
And I would still have these friends
But we would not reflect on how warped I was
During the years you were a part of my life
And I would still have fallen in love again
But it wouldn't have taken as much reassurance
I wouldn't have been so shocked
That love is so different than I thought

What doesn't kill you makes you stronger, sure
But I'd be strong anyway
And the time I spent around you is dead to me
Wasted time

I wish I'd never met you
I wish fate had been paying attention
It was an accident that *wasn't* waiting to happen
It was a calamity, a catastrophe, a mistake

Who I wanted you to be is not who you are
And I'm grieving the loss of the person I wanted
Not the one I got
I mourn the idea of you that I came up with
The person I thought would show up if I just held on
    a little longer
I cry about what *could've* been
If you had been who I wanted you to be
And not who you are

I let a made-up person break my heart

Because if not for the belief in the potential of you
If not for the fictitious traits that made you hard to lose
If not for my complete delusion
If I had seen you for who you are instead of who I hoped
    you'd become
The end would've felt like a triumph
Rather than a grave loss
But I guess the concept of the you I manufactured

Was built on some truth after all

Because I fell in love with a character I made up
Based entirely on being loved *by* you
In the way I already loved you

I woke up one day years later
After the late-night texts
And whispered phone calls
And inconspicuous glances
And standing close, *but not too close*
I woke up one day and realized
The waiting for you to reach out first
The hoping nobody would see me leaving your place
The never going on a real date
Never sharing a meal
Never sober
I woke up and thought about how it was always
Guard up, clothes off
Cab home in the middle of the night
No sleepovers
"That's not what this is" with a kiss on the forehead
That it was only a secret because you were ashamed

Maybe of the situation
Maybe of me
Maybe of yourself

And I can't believe I ever thought love could grow from
    a place of such secrecy
It couldn't
And years later I woke up and realized what it was

But years later I was still thinking about it
And I wonder if you keep thinking about it, too

And that makes me as ashamed now as you were then

I don't worry that you are lying to me
I worry about the way it will feel if I find out you're a liar
I don't worry about the lie itself
I worry about the way the lie will change me
I'm worried that when I find out
My ears will pop
My eyes will glaze over
My stomach will be full of anger
I'm worried I'll be nauseous
And lightheaded
And my eyes will fill while my trust empties
I worry about the moment I find out that I never should've trusted you
While I stand there with cheeks full of words I can't spit out
And I am shaking
And I am now the owner of a heart that will never be the same as it was
The moment before I found out that you are a *liar*
And I am a fool
And that people who love you lie to you

And you might say you wouldn't have had to lie
Had I been more understanding
And I will waver on my worth
And question if it is you or I who is at fault

And I might forgive you
But I will never trust you (or anyone) again

I loved your wandering hands and your wandering dreams
I loved wandering around with you in the city at night
I loved the way that you would wander through thought processes
    until you found answers
And that you seemed just as content being still with me
As some other people felt wandering across the world

But once a wanderer, always a wanderer

Which is probably why your eyes wandered, too
Why your hands wandered to other bodies
And your dreams wandered onto pillows in other people's beds
I wonder how deeply you wandered through your thoughts
    of leaving me
And if you'd ever have done it if I hadn't found out

It must've been naive of me to fall in love with a wanderer
And to still think you were as content with the stillness as you seemed

But all your wandering made me one, too

But for me it was from person to person after you
Because I couldn't trust that none of them would do the things that
    you did
It was back and forth in my apartment going over every time I
    believed you
And feeling so foolish for all of it
From bar to bar with strangers holding hands trying not to bring you
    up after too many drinks

Because a new person's wandering hands don't want to hear about yours,
   or so I've learned

Your wandering left me wandering aimlessly for a long, long time
And wondering, too
If everyone has wanderlust when it comes to relationships
That eventual pull to someplace new and exciting
Or if only the wrong person can bring that out of someone

I think about you all the time

In fever dreams
And goose bumps (the bad kind)
I think about you when it's raining
And when it's too cold
And when it's too hot
And when the road is so slippery I have no control over my car
And I feel like it could be over any second
I think of you when I'm walking alone at night
When I'm in the middle of a really bad flu
When my house is a mess and I don't even know where to start
I think of you when I'm uncomfortable and when I'm scared
When I'm distressed and restless
When I'm ill at ease and unsettled
Not because you'd make it better *but because you made me that way, too*

Those feelings remind me of you

The worst would be to find out that you don't think of me at all
That how you were acting was actually how you felt
That you really did not care
The worst would be to find out that I don't cross your mind
When you pass my exit on the freeway
That when my favorite artist plays in town, you don't wonder if you'll
    run into me at the venue
That when you're at the bar we used to go to
You don't think twice about the potential of my being there, too
That all those cars on the road that look like mine
Don't make you wonder if it's me driving one
You don't find yourself speeding in the lane beside
To get a quick glimpse of whose hands are on the steering wheel
And it really is sad that the worst-case scenario is one
Where you are as unbothered as you always seemed
That you were being honest with me the whole time when
You showed me how indifferent you were

The worst would be to find out that you were telling the truth
    about not caring

While I lied about feeling the same

That you remained unchanged while I went through a character-
    altering event

That you don't think of me at all

You know those abandoned buildings
That are covered in dirt and dust
There's grime and mold and broken glass
And rusty nails and such

There's spray paint with profanities
And boards that block the doors
And you wonder about the people
Who resided there before

How did they make such a mess
Of something that was theirs?
And now it's left deserted
Like they never really cared

And nobody can enter
Even if they wanted to
Those buildings that at one point
Were shiny and brand-new

But now there's just no way to know
The way they used to be
I became that building
The day you were done with me

I trusted you like I trusted cars before I knew what an accident
    felt like
Like I trusted the sun before it burned me badly
Like I trusted my alarm before it didn't go off
I trusted you like I trusted dogs before I was bitten
Like I trusted bikes before I fell off one and cut up my hands
    and knees
I trusted you like I trusted my bones until I fractured one
And realized they aren't quite as strong as I thought
I trusted you like I trusted friends until one betrayed me
Like I trusted walking barefoot on wood until I got a splinter
Like I trusted snow until I realized how beautifully it covers
    black ice
I trusted you like I trusted my heart before I knew what it felt like
    when someone broke it
And trusting you felt like all the things I've trusted and lost trust
    for all at once
It felt like crashing and burning and missing out
Like sunken teeth and open wounds and fractured bones
Like betrayal and pain and spiraling out of control
You broke my heart, and I trusted you not to
I trusted love until I trusted you
And you ruined it

I would take it back in a heartbeat
No questions, no regrets
I would un-meet you
I would undo the whole thing
Without a second thought
I would take back every minute I spent on you
I would give back any of the stories I have to tell
That leave people with their jaws on the table around me as I tell them
I would un-know you so heavily that yours would still be on my list
Of "potential baby boy names" in my Notes app
*But instead I cringe at the handshake of anyone with a name that
    resembles yours*
I would forget all of it
I would say good riddance to everything that came to me because
    of you
Even the good things, which were few and far between
Because there was no lesson to be learned
There was no light at the end of the tunnel
The only good was that it was over
So I would happily have it never happen in the first place

I would take it all back

FRIENDSHIP LOVE

or, The Ones We *Choose*

"I want to marry my best friend"
You say at dinner to the people at the table
As you dream about the great love story that you'll start *eventually*
But haven't found the beginning of yet
You talk to one another about it all the time
How you want love to feel when you *finally find it*
You want it to feel easy and comfortable
Exciting and safe
You say you can't wait to feel that way
You say you want it to feel like you're "marrying your best friend"
How easy to overlook that you only know what it feels like to love
    that way
Because it's the way you *already* love and are loved
By your friends
You're looking for a love that's reminiscent of what you already have
Searching high and low like you don't already have it

Even though I don't know you anymore
I'll always know your heart
And even though we haven't talked in ages
Even if we never talk again
I will always know it's a good one, to its core
That is something I will never question
I know I will be left to wonder a lot of things
Like whether you're happy, or if you still love your job
What makes you stop to watch the whole video on your feed
    before you scroll past it
And how long ago was it that we stopped sending those to each other?
I will wonder where you shop for your clothes, and what your
    kids are really like
I will contemplate what life would've been like had we stayed as
    close as we were
And why we didn't
I guess time is as good a wedge between two people as anything else
But even though I don't know the inner workings of your
    day-to-day
Or of your life at all
I know that heart of yours is still good, and it always will be
And I know all the people in your life now, whom I don't know
    at all
Know it, too
Everything can change; I mean, we did
But your heart won't
It'll be for everyone what it was for me
And I envy all the *now* people and all the *next* people
Who get to have it close by

And I bet they envy me for getting to know it sooner than they did
And even though we didn't stay friends, a good heart stays good
And that's how I know

Being human is being made of your friends
And so much of who you are will be a reflection of them
A mosaic of actions and words and feelings
And you might think that sounds unoriginal
But no single person is made up of all the same people
It's kind of beautiful when you think about it
The phrases you use, the jokes you make
The clothes you like
The way you sing along to songs in the car
The way you react to things
The way you give love, the way you accept it
You mold yourself to be like the people who made you want to be
    more like them
You are made of the friends you find along the way
When you tell stories
When you order your coffee in a specific way
When you show people the party trick you learned from a girl
    you met in college
When you know all the words to a song a friend showed you
    years ago
Or a fun fact that you recite like it has always been yours
But you love getting the reaction from others that you gave
When you heard it for the first time, from your friend
So the next time you're having a hard time with who you are
Think of how hard it is for you to have any hard feelings toward
    the people you love
Because they are the people you're made of
And they are made of you, too

So many of the things you admire about the friends you've found
    along the way
They learned from being friends with you

To the friend who came a little later in life
Thank God you did
Because even though we didn't get to be kids together
We got to grow up together
In exactly the way we needed to at the time
To the friend who became my person
When I was already a whole person
I had already been shaped and shattered
And rebuilt again and again
And you loved all the little imperfections that were left behind
You've even stepped in to reinforce things that broke
Before I met you
I may not have been a part of the story of your foundation
But it is one of my favorite stories to hear about
I love the way we laugh at all that has happened
And the way we take on all that keeps happening
And match our pieces up like a puzzle
We both have carried half of for a long, long time
I love that we chose each other for who we became *without each other*
It makes everything that has ever happened to me feel worth it
And we will never get to know each other "before"
Though somehow I feel like I've never not known you
And I can't imagine a time without you
But now I don't have to
You came around later
But you came at the perfect time
And I think it worked out in just the way it was meant to
Because the grown-up version of me needed you
More than you will ever know

Your friends *choose* to love you
Isn't that something?
They picked you *because* of who you are
Not despite it
Your friends quietly designated you to add to their life without
    asking for a single thing
And you do just that every day, without even trying
They chose you, and it was the *easiest* yes
The kind that slips out when one of you asks to borrow a lip gloss,
    or a charger, or a shirt
A shoulder, or an ear
A thoughtless agreement because it doesn't require any thought at all

Choosing you as a friend was as easy as it is to be around you
Easy like unlocking the door to let them into the passenger seat,
    overusing an inside joke
Making fun of each other for things you *like* being made fun of for
Easy like a conversation over happy-hour margaritas, the same story
    with a new detail
An *"I always feel so good after we hang out"* text
Being your friend feels as if laughter were language
And we finally found someone else who understands
And maybe the choice gets made for us when we choose
    our friends, because the universe knows it would've been
    too hard had we not
As hard as it is to catch your breath when the joke stays funny
    for the whole trip
As hard as the hard moments would be without you to call
It would be hard to not be your friend

And that's why you were my easiest choice
That's why we chose each other
Isn't that something?

It's okay to outgrow a friend
In the same way it's okay to outgrow a pair of jeans that once fit
  you perfectly
And it's okay to be sad about it
Because when you find a friend
A best friend, a favorite friend
One who fits you better than anyone ever has
You don't foresee ever having to let them go
You don't worry about a time when you stop fitting
It's not possible; how could you?
That would be like finding your new favorite pair of jeans
And only thinking about when you have to give them away
Outgrowing something you thought you'd have forever is one of
The most conflicting feelings this life offers you
But the end is rarely sudden
You must do the *growing* in order to *grow apart*
And that takes time

Growing isn't bad, even though we like to demonize it because it
  leads to endings
It leads to things that *used* to fit not fitting anymore
But spending time with friends you've grown out of tends to feel
Uncomfortable, forced, constricted
So you say things like "I'll hang on to this for a little longer just
  in case"

But you are allowed to outgrow your friends
You are allowed to set one another free

While remaining thankful you gave one another exactly what
   you needed at the time
And just like outgrowing your favorite pair of jeans and getting
   new ones
You will see friendships like the one you had with them and say
   to yourself
I used to have a friend like that; I miss them
Knowing full well why you had to let them go
Knowing you just didn't fit each other anymore

And you'll be sad, but you'll be okay

I hope that everybody has the opportunity to have that one friend
At some point in this life
Even if it's just that one time
It doesn't have to last forever; it's okay if you grow apart
I just hope everyone gets to know what it feels like
To even for a moment feel overwhelmingly in tune with someone
Everything matches up, everything makes sense
Everything is funny
Every person deserves a person who makes it fun to do ordinary
    things
Like run an errand or eat Subway sandwiches
Or watch a random rerun of a television show
Or go to the convenience store
Or talk while they swing on swings
Or clean their room while they're on the phone
Or spend the night somewhere new
Someone they can sit in silence with because it feels even more
    comfortable
Than sitting alone
I hope everyone finds that someone at least one time
Because even if it was fleeting, you still got to experience one of
    life's greatest moments of chance
A true soulmate
And if it lasts forever

Well, you're just the luckiest two people in the world, aren't you?

If there's one thing you should look for as an adult
It's sleepover laughter
The kind of laughter you felt as a kid when you were delirious
The lights were off
You had been warned one too many times by whoever's parents
    that it was time to be quiet
You're not sure what time it is
But you're pretty sure this is the latest you've ever stayed up in
    your life
You're lying on somebody's floor with a blanket draped over you
It's covered in some cartoon character you're beyond familiar with
You're pretty sure you have the same blanket in your basement, too
And you are laughing so hard there are tears rolling down your face
You are curled up with uncontrollable joy
Any sound that leaves anyone's mouth within proximity
Sounds like the most carefully planned, well-rehearsed comedy
    routine ever written
Your stomach hurts because you cannot stop laughing
Sleepover laughter
That's what you should be looking for now
Moments that make you feel exactly like that
And people who make you laugh exactly like that

It doesn't happen as often as it used to, so when it does
I hope you notice

Sometimes I find it funny when a friend asks me if they can borrow
    a sweater
Or a lip gloss or a pair of earrings
I find it amusing when they ask for a ride home
Or if I can get this one, and they'll get the next
It's always a little comical when they ask to borrow a phone charger
    or a hair tie
Or if they can have a snack, or water from my fridge
And it's always with a little bit of uncertainty
Like they've just asked for something so grand
Always followed up with an explanation or an apology
And I find it funny, because I don't know if they know how small the
    things they ask for are
In comparison to the limits of the things that I *would* do for them
I don't even know if the limit exists
Because I'd let them borrow my organs if they needed them
I'd let my heart beat for them
I think it already does
They don't need to give me the reason because they *are* the reason
Because I would pretty much do anything for them if they needed me to

And it would be a stretch to say all friendships are this way
But our friendship is this way

So yes, of course you can

Girlhood is magic, you see

Because girls are shape-shifters

They become whatever you need them to be, and that is what
girlhood is

They shift into bridesmaids and bartenders

And comedians and therapists

And soulmates and sisters

And soft places to land and givers of tough love

There are many things in this life I could've done without,
but not girls

I couldn't do it without them

They're magic

Girlhood is magic

I compare myself to you all the time
I compare my body to your body
My hair to your hair, my clothes to your clothes
And I wish to be you in all those ways
But when we make each other laugh, I don't wish to be more like you
I am so glad that you're you and I'm me
Because that's what makes us so funny together
And when we share secrets, I don't wish to be more like you
Because I love the way we trust each other
And when we make each other feel less alone, I don't wish to be
    more like you
Because I am so glad both of us are there
We need each other in different ways because we're different people
So instead of saying "I wish I looked like you"
I should say "I'm glad my heart is like yours"
Instead of saying "I wish I wore that same outfit"
I should say "I'm glad our senses of humor fit so perfectly"
Instead of saying "I wish my hair looked that way"
I should say "It's amazing how two souls can align this way"
But for some reason, I sit here thinking I'd be a better me if I *looked*
    like you
But if I were you in the ways I wish to be, there wouldn't be an us
And sometimes I forget that I am a part of the beautiful equation
    we've become
There is beauty in the both of us

Sometimes I can't believe we're not friends anymore
I always thought it would take something radical for that to happen
Something completely unforgivable, and even then I would probably
Still have forgiven you
I thought it would take something abysmal to tear us apart
That we would have to go up in flames, and even then I would
    probably stay to collect the ashes
But it turned out that time would do it kindly and gently
And so slowly we wouldn't notice until it was too late
Like two ships anchored in calm water
And the anchors lifted, and we drifted and
We both stayed afloat, even apart
I still can't believe we're not friends anymore
Because we were once experts in each other
We did everything together
And I had no idea that growing up can mean growing apart
    simultaneously
This isn't the way we planned it, is it
We were the definition of comfortable silence and breathless laughter
    and infinite trust
We knew each other by heart
We were exactly what each other needed at the time
And I never thought I would put the word "were" before the word
    "friends" when it comes to you
But I do now when I talk about you, and I still can't believe it
But I find solace in knowing that, when I miss who I was before
That version of me is alive within you, because it's the only one you'll
    ever know
I'll be her to you forever

And I hope you know the same is true for me
Which is beautiful, and awful, because I'd love to know you now
But if all I can have is *were* and not *are*
I'll just be grateful that I had a friendship
Like that at all
So much of who I am is because of who we were when we were
    friends
So everyone who knows me and everyone who knows you
Kind of knows us
But not like we knew each other
And just as often as I wonder how it happened
I wonder how you're doing
And I really hope you're well

You're not *just* a girl
You're the best friend I've ever had
You're not *just* anything
You're everything
Knowing you has healed me in a way I think you understand
Because knowing me has healed you, too

I have always known love exists
Because of the way I love my friends
I know because even during my biggest and most harrowing
    heartbreaks
Love was all around me
It was in phone calls and text messages
It was in happy-hour margaritas
And borrowed outfits and the retrieval of stray eyelashes
It was in fitness classes and at the bottom of coffee cups
In my passenger seat and sprawled out on couches
It was in deep belly laughter when I thought I would never
    smile again
Some of the most agonizing endings have never left me with
    an absence of love
They always leave me with more, somehow
More proof that love is real
Because of them, heartache has always left me running
Into the arms of the love that never hesitates to make itself known
I have said goodbye to love again and again
I have watched it end slowly and abruptly
I have thought it was love when it wasn't
I have loved so hard without being loved in return
And I have never wavered on knowing for sure that love always
    prevails
And it's because of the way I love my friends

I hope we're best friends in the next life, too
And in every universe before and after this one
We find each other
I hope in every world I can call you
And in every hard thing you are there with me
I hope in every lifetime we meet
I don't care how or when—*I just hope it happens*
Because I want every universe to feel the way you make this one feel
Whatever comes next, I want to walk in, scan the room, and find you
And we will sit across from each other
And drink espresso martinis
And be ready for *whatever it is*
I hope in the next life we don't just cross paths but walk the same one
That you are always there to tell me what you're going to wear
And to send me podcast-length voice notes
Because it means that all lives will be as good as this life
Because I will always have a best friend
Who's as good at being my best friend as you are

Being a long-distance friend didn't feel like as hard a choice as it
    turned out to be
When I was making the decision to do it
I said goodbye to the people I loved the most
And moved to another time zone
And now everything we do is divided by just a couple of hours
And a few thousand miles
But it feels like more than that
Because before it was just literal distance, and now it's figurative, too
Now we're divided by dozens of bottles of wine I wasn't there to share
And happy-birthday FaceTimes instead of happy-birthday hugs
And sending gifts to their babies in the mail
Signing the cards "I cannot wait to watch you grow," knowing it will
    be through a screen
I swear I still feel like we're just kids
And now they have kids of their own
And I am missing all of it
We're divided by expensive flights
And missed calls
"Will you be home for Christmas?" texts
And "Hoping to make it to the next one" replies
I'm seeing engagement rings on Instagram instead of in person
And wishing with every bone in my body that I had the luxury of just
    stopping by on a whim, being around for not just the big things but
    also the small things
Joining that random Thursday-night dinner with the friends who feel
    like home
The friends who live at home, *while I don't*
The house I grew up in still stands tall

And my mom still answers the landline
My childhood bedroom exactly as I left it
Me a different person every time I spend the night
Because the distance between the times I make it home gets longer
    and longer
Although I use the word "home" to describe two places now
And when my friends ask "Do you think you'll ever be back for good?"
While we hug in the driveway before I leave again for the airport
My answer has varied over the years
But I think I've always known I would be the long-distance friend forever
And it never gets easier

Always a bridesmaid, never a bride
But why is that a bad thing?
Being a bridesmaid means you found one of the loves of your life
Isn't that the whole point?
The thing we're always told to do?
Find a love that never goes away
That is what this is
Always a bridesmaid, never a bride
Meant to describe a person who hasn't reached their full potential
A person in the making
I'm making it just fine, and it's because of her
Always there when you need her most
Always answers the phone
Always a reminder of what love really is
In all ways I will always be proud
To be a bridesmaid

SELF-LOVE

or, *The One Who Matters Most*

———

This comeback is personal
And it's for me, not you
Maybe it's because of you, but it's about me
And maybe I lost sight of the fact that it should've *always*
    been about me
But I remember now that I've come back to life
And the color has returned to my face
Now that every day isn't overcast with a chance of
    someone getting in my way
This revival is mine
And I don't even care if you see it
Because I see it, *finally*
I see potential in *me* instead of *you*
I know I will keep getting better and better
I don't just have to sit around and hope for it
Because I will not disappoint myself in the way that I've
    been disappointed
This comeback is personal
After falling backward or lying stagnant
I'm past moving on; I'm moving forward for me and with me
Using all the strength I forgot about for all that time
Turns out you can save it up for as long as you want, and it turns
    into a second wind
A bounce back
The kind of confidence that makes people uncomfortable
And I'd say watch me, *but I'd rather you didn't*
Because this might be *about* you, but it isn't *for* you

It's for me

You say you miss the old you
But where do you think you went
Every you you've ever been is in there
Like ingredients in a recipe coming together beautifully
Rather than starting from scratch, over and over
You say you miss the old you
As if that version of you is at the party and you're in the bathroom
Just faintly hearing the music from afar
But that's not the case at all
If you weren't so busy looking everywhere but within you for the
    person you used to be
You'd be at the party, too
The old you is still you
You do not need to grieve
You do not need to say goodbye or write a eulogy
You just need to pull up another chair for who you are now
Sit in harmony with who you've been and make room later for who
    you become
And you will find that there are things you don't agree upon
And traits you don't favor
But just because those versions have been outgrown *doesn't mean*
    they're gone
You say you miss the old you, but you haven't gone anywhere

It's a party you're at, not a funeral

I woke up today and looked in the bathroom mirror
And started picking out the parts of me that I wish were *better*
I wished my arms were thinner and my skin was clearer
I wished my stomach was flatter and my legs more toned
I wished my hair was longer
And that I looked better in glasses *so I wouldn't have to wear contacts
    all the time*
I put my jeans on and wished they fit me better
Slipped on a shirt and questioned it, *as I do*
Then I went about my day, and wished myself away some more
I wished away parts of me in window reflections and car mirrors
I wished I looked as good as another woman I saw at the gas station
I realized I forgot my headphones and wished my brain didn't let me
    down so frequently
I wished that winter made me a little less sad
And that I could eat whatever I wanted, while I ate a cucumber
    instead of fries
I wished for a nicer car and a cleaner house
I wished for so much to change
But if I were offered a chance to wish for a different life than this one
I would politely decline and ask to keep it
Because it has been *mostly* wonderful to me
A little contradictory, isn't it?
And a little overwhelming
How many things we wish to change every single day
But I still wish tomorrow will be a little different from today
Because tomorrow I'll wish to be a little more grateful
That I am a wishful thinker
With a life that, if given the chance, I wouldn't wish away

You're worthy now, you know
In this moment, as you are
Even if you didn't shower today
If you didn't shave your legs
If your house is a mess
If your skin is covered in blemishes and stretch marks
If the number on your scale is too high for your liking
You're worthy right now
If you were late for work
And your hair isn't clean
Or your clothes aren't fitting right
If you stared at yourself in the mirror in that bathing suit for a little
    too long at the store
Or you can't afford any of the beauty products you saw online today
You're still worthy
Even if there's something else you feel like you should be doing
If you're being betrayed or taken advantage of
If someone forgot it's your birthday
Or you're riddled with regret about something you can't take back
You're worthy if you don't like any of your clothes and have nothing
    to wear
If your car is falling apart
If your nails need doing
If your house looks different from someone else's
If your life does, too
If your stomach scrunches over your waistband while you're sitting
If you never read books
If you haven't been cooking at home enough
If you feel like a bad parent

Or you need your parents
Or you miss your parents
Or you didn't have the kind of parents you deserved
If you feel like you're too far gone
If no one has reminded you of your worth
This is your reminder
You are worthy
Right now

There's more to celebrate than rings

And babies

And buying a house

And it would be a real shame not to live that way

Because if those things are behind you, it feels *over*

And if they're ahead of you, it feels *far*

And if they're not in the cards

It can make you feel unworthy, *but you're not*

Because there is so much to celebrate

And we should do it more

We should glorify endings the same way we do beginnings

Because they are beginnings in disguise

We should throw big parties when someone walks away from the
   wrong person

The same way we did when they found them

And gather together for people

When they choose themselves and cheer them on

We should acknowledge anniversaries of friendships

And the day we got our pet

And write people cards *just because we can*

Just because we have them and they're here

Why would we not be celebrating that

It's like there's this quintessential list of things

That deserve big ceremonies and observances

They deserve balloons and flowers

And loud proclamations

But in case no one has told you

Getting out of bed after a while of not being able to

Is worth revelry

And finding peace on your own
Is party-worthy
Deciding to do what's best for you
Should be showered with joy
And just because your moment isn't on that list
Doesn't mean it shouldn't be commended
There are so many things to celebrate in life
And you should celebrate all of them

I know you love to dwell on the past
But nothing new can grow there
No matter how many times you replay it, it will not change
Like those movies you watch again and again
I know the thoughts of the things that have already happened make
    you feel safe
Because you can be sure of them
But there are so many parts that you wish to change, and you can't
It's impossible
Nothing that has already happened can happen differently
Nothing new can grow in any moment earlier than this one

If you want to change something, it can't be yesterday

What already happened is meant for reminiscing about
But you are *longing*
You're yearning, you're hungry, and you're itching to go back
But you can't
So stop being mad at yourself for yesterday
And make the decision you wish you'd made then, now

I know you love to dwell on the past
But nothing new can grow there
Nothing new can grow there

Loving *you* is not the hard part of love

Love can be hard sometimes

But you are not hard to love

And if anyone makes you feel like *you* are the complicated,
  taxing part of love

(The part that is inevitable every once in a while, because if
  it were easy everyone would do it forever)

Then it probably isn't love it all

Being in love with *you* is not the hard part

It will never be the hard part

What if you could pull the shame out of yourself
Like a loose thread on a T-shirt you've worn too many times
Quickly like a strip of wax, or the stinger of a wasp, or a Band-Aid
What if you could pull the shame out of the very fiber of who you
   are *just like that*
And why can't you; *why don't you*
For so many of the things you are ashamed of aren't shameful at all
They just make you who you are
And they make you just like everybody else
But not in a way that's unoriginal
Just in a way that you're not alone
And I'm not saying you should never be ashamed
I just think you're placing shame where it doesn't belong
And if you tied all your misplaced humiliation together
Like the kind you feel about your personal success
Or your financial situation
The kind you feel about your perfectly adequate body
Or the direction your thoughts take you in from time to time
The kind of shame you feel when you run out of capacity
And when your jeans are too tight
Or you order fries when you told yourself you'd get a salad
When you're not as far along as you thought you'd be
When you're sad on a sunny day
The kind of shame that everybody tries to shove into a closet as
   quickly as possible
Before guests show up so they won't know what a mess it is
Even though your visitors have closets and drawers in a constant state
   of disarray all the same

And you'll likely still utter the words "Sorry for the mess"
As if you're the only one who doesn't have it all figured out
We're all riddled with shame over things that only deserve to be met
With empathy and grace; we just don't talk about it
And if we did, it wouldn't be shameful, *it would just be*
What if we strung all that shame together and then pulled it out of you
Quickly and painlessly
So you could feel something else for a change

It's hard to feel sparkly again after someone takes it away
Whether *someone* is them or *someone* is you
It's not easy to get it back, but you can, you know
And you will
Even if it feels like looking for house keys you can't remember
    putting down
Or defogging the windows of a car that's out of gas
Or a spur-of-the-moment haircut taking forever to grow back
A hopeless feeling with no immediate fix
But when it happens, you will *know*
Like when you wake up and *know* your lingering sickness has fully
    disappeared
It will be as much of a relief as taking a cool shower after a long day
    in the hot sun
And as obvious as the sparkle of a diamond ring right after it's
    polished
All of it is brighter than you ever remember it being
And only you will know it happened at first
But everyone else will know it soon, too
Because you will sparkle like *you* again
Inward, outward, and onward
You will get it back because it's yours
And it was never gone, just misplaced
It was hiding with your house keys
It was waiting for you at the gas station
It took a while to come back, but it's back
It always comes back

I don't think I've ever broken anyone's heart in the way I've had my
heart broken

I can't imagine anyone canceling plans in hopes that I would reach out
to ask them to come over *even if it were in the middle of the night*

I can't picture someone rolling over and lighting their phone up again
and again

Hopelessly waiting for my reply

I don't know that anyone has ever said "I can fix her, and then she will
love me"

And known all the pain would be worth it if the day comes when I
change my mind

I'm pretty certain no one has ever cried all the way home after leaving
my place

Wondering if our brief physical exchanges would ever make them
feel less numb after

Less heartbroken, *less desperate*

I don't think anyone has ever been jealous of the people I pay
attention to

Frantically scrolling through their Instagram pages

Comparing themselves, asking "*What do they have that I don't*"

"*Why them and not me*"

"*I would do anything to be wanted by her the way I want her*"

I don't think anyone has ever inconsolably and irrevocably yearned
for me

In a way that alters a period of their life so much that they talk to
their therapist about it

But I also don't have it in me to put someone through that

I don't think I have a thread strong enough to let someone
    hang from it
In the way that I've been hung
I don't think I lack awareness in the way I would have to
To let someone hurt in the way that I've hurt
And now that I'm thinking about it
I don't think any of the times my heart has been broken
    in the way that it has
Were ever truly accidents
I think both of us knew it was happening
And I just don't have it in me to do it in return

I didn't know it at the time

But loving *me* was letting *you* go

And hindsight allows me to see the hardest thing I've ever done
as something beautiful

Because not choosing you anymore *was* choosing me

I'm *almost* happy
And I think that's more than enough
Maybe that's what we should start asking people
Instead of "Are you happy"
Are you almost happy
Are you getting close
Are you at the blissful part of the trip when you know you're *just
about there*
The part where the scenery is memorable
And you're excited but kind of tired
You're anxious, *in a good way*
The part right before you have to lift the heavy bags out of the car
Almost happy
Like when the rain is close to clearing
So you're really enjoying the last of it before the clouds move
completely
Like if you got home any sooner, your favorite song wouldn't have
time to finish
So you slow down a little and wait before turning off the engine
There's always going to be something
At least for me, anyway
Something that keeps full happiness at arm's length
But I'm more than okay with almost
Maybe, like many things in life
There's a thrill in the chase of true happiness
And I think I'd be a little bored if I made it to the peak, *because
then what*
I'll be looking for more anyway
Because it's in my blood to always be slightly dissatisfied

It would be a shame if there were nothing left to find
Keep the map on
I'm enjoying the trip
I like being *almost* there
So the next time someone asks me if I'm happy
I will smile and say "Almost"
And I think they will say "Me, too"

One of these times it's going to stick
You're going to start and never stop
And it's going to change your life
One of these times it's going to work
And you won't even remember the way it was before
Because it's so good now
And it's all going to be because of *you*
You're the only one who could ever stop you
And one of these times, you won't
And you'll have only yourself to thank
One of these times will make the way it *is* become the way it *was*
And it might not be the next time, but it'll definitely be one of
    the times
Not everything is doomed to end
And you are not destined for mediocrity the way you think you are
So never stop starting
Because that's the only way it'll work

Just because your body looks *different*
Doesn't mean your body looks *bad*
Just because you scrolled up in your camera roll
And you used to look smaller
Doesn't mean the way you look now is wrong
What if you celebrated all the living that led to a bigger body
Because if you had never known anything but the way you are now
You would not be so hard on yourself
And I fear if we don't learn to love our bodies even as they get bigger,
    as they change
We will spend forever wishing away who we *are* in pursuit of who
    we *were*
Because I know you didn't love the body you wish you could get back,
    did you?
I know you've always wished to be different
And wished to be smaller
And wished to take up less space
And you've always scrolled back to old photos
And wished to go back in time
But you can't
And if you don't learn to stop being ashamed of your body today
Well, that will be the biggest shame of all
Because time will not stop for you to give you more days to hate
    yourself
It will keep passing, and you will wish you took new photos instead
    of fixating on the old ones
You will wish you spent more time in bathing suits feeling the water
    against your skin
And less time worrying what you looked like while you did it

Just because your body has changed
Doesn't mean your body is bad
You have to believe me
Because you're running out of time to enjoy your beautiful body

I didn't have fun 'cause I thought I looked fat
It ruined my night; was as simple as that
Everyone else ate and drank, danced and laughed
I drowned in self-pity 'cause I thought I looked fat

I didn't have fun 'cause my jeans felt too tight
You may think there's no way, but you heard me just right
I hated my body; it ruined my night
I could've had fun, but my jeans felt too tight

I deleted the photos 'cause of how my arms looked
Just an ounce of self-hatred was all that it took
Not as small as they are in my made-up rule book
I deleted the photos 'cause of how my arms looked

My best friend married her soulmate last year
I stood by her side, wanted to disappear
'Cause my dress got tighter as her wedding neared
I made her day about me in my head last year

And now I see photos of when my jeans felt small
And I wish for the body I had then after all
'Cause the only thing ever too big or too tall
Is the standard I set for myself to be small

It wasn't from my body that my worth ever stemmed
If it was, well, I wouldn't miss how I looked then
It's just a dysmorphic state of ill intent
Hating my body like it's some kind of trend

I looked at old photos and missed who I was
And wondered which photos were missing because
My brain doesn't stop with the thing that it does
So I hate who I am while I miss who I was

Your big emotions are what make you *remember*
So before you wish you were someone who could level out more often
Or stay calm or be cool or not be so anxious
Try to think of the last time you recalled a day you felt nothing
Because it's the moments that left your hands shaking
Or your eyes watering
Or your stomach full of butterflies
That you'll have the most trouble forgetting about
And I don't think that's a bad thing
Even if what made something memorable was crying all the way home
Or laughing so hard that the people at the tables around you were
    rolling their eyes
Calling someone you shouldn't have because the band played that
    one song
And your whole body had to dial their number
Speaking to a crowd while your heart was beating out of your chest
Meeting someone new for the first time
And hoping they don't notice your quivering water glass as you lift it
    to meet your lips
Fighting with someone at the top of your lungs in a way that either
    made you or broke you
All those feelings make moments matter so much more than they
    would've
If you didn't feel them the way that you do
Big emotions turn our very limited days from tedious to remarkable
Don't ever be ashamed of the way you turn the corners in on the pages
    of your life
So you can go back to them
And remember exactly how they felt

What if the day never comes that you stop hating your body so much
What if the end comes—and it will—
And you forgot to learn to love yourself, and suddenly it's too late
And you spent all your good days wishing to be different
And now you're left wishing that you hadn't been blind to how
  beautiful you'd been all along
Because you will never look back and be glad you said those awful
  things about your body
That you wore long sleeves
That you deleted those photos
That you skipped that meal
That you held on to those smaller jeans
You won't wish you weighed less at that event
That your legs looked more toned on that vacation
That you'd stayed in that calorie deficit for longer
That you shouldn't have ordered those fries that day at the beach
You won't think any of those things
You will never want a moment back once it's gone and you're at
  the end
So you can feel skinny in it
You will want it back to feel everything else
You will run out of time to hate yourself because you will run out of
  time for everything
You will run out of time—that's a guarantee
And you are wasting time wishing to be someone else, to be some
  other way
Because you will miss being this way when the end comes—
  and it will
You will miss the way you were in that photo you deleted

The way you were when you thought you'd rather be any other way
And you will hate yourself for hating yourself when you could've
  just lived with yourself
And loved yourself
When there is no time left to do any of it

Anxiety and I do everything together
That sounds better than saying I do everything with anxiety
But I do
Everything
We wake up and go to sleep *together*
We think everyone hates us *together*
I hate us together
But we're roommates; we live together
Although some days it doesn't feel much like living
It feels more like unease and discomfort
And struggling through conversations
And wondering if I said too much or too little
Or the wrong thing altogether
It doesn't feel like living; it feels like floating, but heavily
And hunger with no appetite
And butterflies, but bad ones
It feels like I'm dying, and anxiety agrees
So we panic and ruminate together
We google it all day long
We sleep too much and then sleep too little
And both make it worse, not better
And we call it living
We have the kind of relationship I would urge anyone I love to work on
Not leave but work on
Because too much time with anything is bound to make you sick of it
    eventually
And I'm sick of it, and sick with it
But stuck with it all the same
Like a bad memory or a bad habit

And when I don't feel it, I feel unbalanced
I wonder where it went until it comes back
And then I feel like me again, somehow
I think anxiety and I may always do everything together, *or most things,*
anyway
So I will keep doing things anyway
Because even if we're doing it together, we've got to live

If you can't change it today, don't waste the day away wishing it
were different
Because right now it is what it is
It can't be different; it won't, not today
And if you want it to change, that's okay
You're allowed to alter your life whenever you want in whichever
way you choose
But change takes time
So to sit and wallow in hating the way something is and wishing
instead that it was not
Well, that is a waste of your time
And a cruel punishment to your mind and your heart
You cannot go back in time and alter your route to change the way
today is
But you *can* decide about tomorrow
And this isn't tomorrow, it's now
And you can't get it back
So don't spend it recklessly
Like you're tossing a hundred-dollar bill into a wishing well that
would've accepted a penny
And your wish would be equally as likely to come true either way
Change is slow and steady
And you can start today, but don't miss today
Things can be different, and they will be
So instead of the constant argument between you and yourself
about all you haven't done
Have a conversation over coffee about all you're capable of
All you can do
All that is to come

I am a people pleaser to my core.

I just want to make everybody happy, but in my constant need to fulfill everyone's happiness, I lose mine. It happens all the time. *We're all just people, you see.* There is no defining thing that makes someone more important than another, or anyone more important than you, though we spend all our lives prioritizing other people and never ourselves. Who cares what I think about me when I can worry about what they think about me instead? Who cares what I need when I can fulfill what *they* need? And one of my greatest fears would be that they are also choosing me and not them, and I'm not even noticing; I'm not even grateful for it. Because it's not just me who's like this, it's you, too. The people who would do anything for anyone but them. A revolving door of discomfort for the comfort of another person, and no one even acknowledges it. And as the world spins on and I keep you happy, and vice versa, I want you to make a deal.

I'll choose me if you choose you.

But you first; I insist.

You're allowed more than one success story
More than one triumph
More than one comeback
You're allowed to change your life again and again and again
And it never gets less impressive
You are allowed endless resurgences
And as many revivals as you want
You can change your life over and over
And it will always be magnificent every single time
There's no limit to the number of times you're allowed to fail
And certainly no limit to how many times you can get back up again
Doing it once doesn't mean you can't do it again
It means you can, and there's proof
Wake up that part of you and do it again
Have another comeback
You will always be welcome at the finish line
And there will always be a roar waiting for you when you get there
You are allowed more than one success story
Do it again and again and again

When you spend your whole life trying to be *smaller*
You forget about the other *small* things that matter way more than
    how *small* you are
I've walked downtown streets on perfect autumn days
The kind I waited all year for
And I missed the moment I deserved to have because I caught a
    glimpse of my body
In a store window and I didn't look *small* enough
And that felt bigger to me than anything else
I've been on airplanes to other worlds and back again
And instead of excitement I felt dismay toward the seat belt
When there wasn't quite as much extra strap as there was the last time
And sure, I could focus on the trip I just went on
But are these armrests tighter against my thighs than they were seven
    days ago?
I've spent days on sandy beaches and immersed in the clearest blue
    water
Surrounded by beauty as far as the eye can see, and felt momentary bliss
Until I had to leave the water
Until I had to feel my not-small thighs trudge through waves
While I wished myself *smaller and smaller*
Or at least small enough that maybe no one would look at me while I
    walked back to my towel
And wrapped myself up in it as tightly as I could until I disappeared
I've been treated poorly by people and still wanted to be more like
    them, *not in heart but in size*
I've stood beside women whose friendships are some of the greatest
    loves I've ever known
While they marry the loves of their lives and deleted the photos

Because my arms weren't small enough
I've watched movies that win Academy Awards in theaters with
people I love
And only wished *my* body looked like *her* body when I took my
clothes off
And that I'd said no when they offered extra butter
Why did I say yes to that? Why didn't I order a small?
I've not bought a perfect pair of jeans because the size that fit wasn't
small enough
Tried on smaller shoes for the sake of no one hearing me ask for my
real size
Whispered my weight to the lady at the DMV in my smallest voice
So no one would ever know I admitted out loud that I'm not as small
as I'd like to be
And I fear that my smallness will never be a small thing, and always
the *biggest* thing
And somehow that fear still doesn't outweigh my fear of not being small
For I've gone to funerals of people I love and still taken a moment to
hate my body
In my black dress
Felt proud of myself on days when I ate smaller portions
Been congratulated for looking smaller
And been applauded for making my personality smaller, too
And one day when there are a small number of days left
And I look back to the days when there were many ahead
There won't even be a small part of me that is thankful for how greatly
I cared
About any of my smallness

You shouldn't have to feel brave to show your body
You shouldn't have to muster courage to take your towel off
    at the pool
And jump into the water
You shouldn't need an all-encompassing sense of fearlessness
To wear shorts on a hot day
I wish you didn't need a strong will to show your stretch marks
And that you didn't need to build up your confidence
To keep the lights on in your bedroom
On the off chance that your body might change someone's mind
I wish you didn't have to be bold to post a photo that shows
    your cellulite
Or daring to look at the scale at the doctor's office
I wish that being a human with a body
Didn't have a prerequisite of being brave
Because there are so many things in this life that you have to face
And so many situations that require you to be tough
Your energy is needed in so many other ways every single day
Yet here we are, needing a brave face
And a brave body to go along with it
I hope one day we can save our courage for things that actually
    require it
We can set aside our fearlessness for setting boundaries
And our strong will for doing hard things like getting through
    the day
We can use our confidence to spread light and have meaningful
    conversations
And our boldness to tell people how we really feel

And let our bodies be bodies
The way they were always meant to

I think living like that would be the bravest thing we could ever do

I'm addicted to trying to change everything about me
I am fully dependent on the idea that one day I will be different
And have lost complete control over being okay with who I am
I have an obsession with the things that are *wrong* with me
And the list of my personal shortcomings is much longer than
The list of things about me that I actually like
I think about changing myself all day, every day
It's the first thing I think of when I wake up
And the last thing I think of before I go to bed
I have an addiction to struggling with who I am
And some may say it's good to have goals
But these aren't goals, they are mandatory for my self-worth
And they exist in a never-ending loop
Because no change is ever enough to make me want to stay still
    and just be who I am
I have been addicted to things before, and I have moved past them
I have put a wrench in many nasty habits
But this seems to be the hardest of them all to quit
And it is the greatest paradox of all
That my deep-rooted need to change everything about me
Is the one thing I want to change the most

I don't think about anything as much as I think about my body
Everybody has a body
But I feel so alone in the way I feel about mine
I feel so alone when every piece of clothing from my closet is
    scattered across every inch of my bedroom and I'm in tears
    because it's not the clothes, it's my body, and I can't get a new
    one like I can get a new shirt
I feel so alone when I get to the party and I keep going to the
    bathroom and looking at myself in the mirror from the side
I feel so alone in my body while I stand naked on a scale in my
    bathroom and wonder why I am always so out of control
While I scroll up in my camera roll with a pit in my stomach,
    looking at photos of the body I hated and wishing I could
    have it, I feel alone

I watch the bodies of everyone around me change with age
    and think it is beautiful for everyone except me
I give everyone grace and I give myself unrelenting criticism
I feel alone while I curse the lighting in changing rooms
And while I pinch at my stomach in the morning as I brush
    my teeth
I feel alone while I stare at my legs next to my friends' legs
    in the back of the cab and feel put off by the size of them
While I'm at the gym and I can feel my stomach fold over
    my leggings
The way I feel about my body is lonely and it is all-encompassing
    and it is all the time
And I know there is so much more that matters

And I know there is no one I love for the way they look; it is
    always only for the way they are
And maybe one day I will learn to see me the way I see
    everyone else
Because everybody has a body
A strong, capable, beautiful body that has nothing to do with
    the way they are
But I feel so alone in the way I feel about mine

Hey, you're good
Please know that you're good
Even if today left you misunderstood
And if nothing came from doing all that you could
I promise it's cool, I promise you're good

Hey, you're fine
Believe me, you're fine
You've been this low before, *like plenty of times*
If you're thinking you're not, well, this is your sign
I promise you're good, I promise you're fine

Hey, you're strong
Please know that you're strong
I know you've been challenged a little too long
But where you are now is right where you belong
You're good, you're fine, I promise you're strong

Hey, it's cool, believe me, it's cool
I know this life can seem so petty and cruel
But one day all this will seem so minuscule
You're good, you're fine, you're strong, and you're cool

Hey, you're *you*
Right there, that's the proof
Look at the maps of the things you've been through
Look at the beauty you've turned it into
You're doing so good, just keep being you

Hey, you're good
Because life is so good
You've made it through times you never thought you would
Look at the craziness that you've withstood
Just stay on the ride; everything's good

ACKNOWLEDGMENTS

It would take a really long time to name every person I've ever loved and acknowledge them in the way they deserve, good or bad—but if I have loved you, thank you. No matter where we stand, how it started, or how it ended (if it did), I'm eternally grateful. I fall in love all the time, with everything, and I used to find it a detriment, but now I finally view it as a blessing. As it turns out, I'm not the only one who holds on to these big feelings. I'm grateful for anyone who has given me a place to put them.

Stephen, when this book is finally out in the world, you'll be my husband—and there is truly no one else I'd rather spend a lifetime pouring all my love into. Thank you for never running out of space for all of it. I'm so endlessly grateful that I get to love you.

Mom, you raised me in an "I love you" house, and it has echoed into the rest of my life in the very best ways. Thank you for telling me you love me a million times a day, every day, while I was growing up. I hope you know the impact it had, and how deeply I know you meant it.

If this book were allowed to be longer, I would list all the friends who make writing about friendship so easy. You know who you are, and I'm so happy we chose each other. I hope we find each other in every lifetime.

To my agent and editor, Kelly and Ronnie—you have truly changed my life. Thank you for giving me a space to pour all my feelings onto pages, and for your sharp, thoughtful guidance on every word. I know I've said I fall in love quickly and easily, so believe me when I say I genuinely love you both. Thank you for everything.

ABOUT THE AUTHOR

Josie Balka is a broadcaster, voice-over artist, and poet. She holds a diploma in radio, television, and film from Niagara College and has worked for some of the largest media companies in North America as an on-air personality. She can often be caught recording viral poetry in her soundproof closet. She was born and raised in Toronto and currently lives in Calgary, Alberta, Canada. She is the author of the *New York Times* bestselling *I Hope You Remember* and *Loves of Our Lives*. Follow her on Instagram @JosieBalka.

ABOUT THE TYPEFACE

Adobe Caslon is part of the Adobe Originals program, which creates high-quality, historically influenced digital typefaces. Designed for on-screen readability in 1990 by Carol Twombly, Adobe Caslon is directly inspired by the Old-Style serif created by William Caslon in 1722. Caslon is often chosen for poetry typesetting thanks to its graceful handling of white space and warm, humanistic rhythm on the page, making it easier to read in longer stretches.